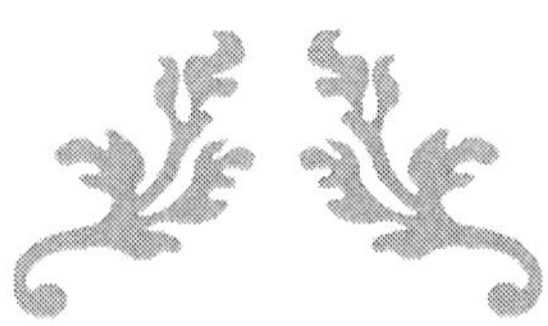

UNDERSTANDING THE SUSTAINABLE DEVELOPMENT GOALS (SDGS) -A COMPREHENSIVE GUIDE

Dr. Mahapara Abbass, Dr. Uzma Abbas & Dr. Shalom Akhai

Understanding the Sustainable Development Goals (SDGs) - A Comprehensive Guide

By

Dr. Mahapara Abbass
Department of Civil Engineering, Maharishi Markandeshwar Engineering College,
Maharishi Markandeshwar (Deemed to be University), Mullana, Ambala, Haryana –
133207, India.

Dr. Uzma Abbass
Dogra Law College
Bari Brahmana, Duggar, Jammu, Indian

Dr. Shalom Akhai
Department of Mechanical Engineering, Maharishi Markandeshwar Engineering
College, Maharishi Markandeshwar (Deemed to be University), Mullana, Ambala,
Haryana – 133207, India.

Highbrow Scribes Publications
Rohini, Delhi, India.

Understanding The Sustainable Development Goals (SDGs) - A Comprehensive Guide

Dr Mahapara Abbass, Dr Uzma Abbass & Dr Shalom Akhai

Published 2024 by Highbrow Scribes Publications

Printed in New Delhi, India

ISBN: 978-81-980325-6-0

Highbrow Scribes Publications's mission is to foster a universal passion for reading by partnering with authors to help create stories and communicate ideas that inform, entertain, and inspire, and to connect them with readers everywhere.

Highbrow Scribes Publications books are printed on acid-free paper.

www.highbrowscribes.com

Preface

The journey of humanity towards sustainable development is not merely a goal but a necessity for our survival and the well-being of future generations. With the Sustainable Development Goals (SDGs), we have a comprehensive framework to address global challenges such as poverty, inequality, climate change, and environmental degradation. This book is a humble attempt to shed light on these pressing issues, offering readers a consolidated resource to understand and act on the SDGs. We have strived to contribute to the betterment of society and the upliftment of humanity. This book has been crafted with the hope that it will inspire individuals, communities, and organizations to embrace sustainable practices and become agents of positive change. By learning about the SDGs, readers can understand their pivotal role in creating a world that is equitable, inclusive, and resilient.

Disclaimer: This book presents information and perspectives gathered from various sources. While every effort has been made to ensure accuracy, the authors do not claim that this book is entirely free from errors or omissions. The views and interpretations presented here are the authors' own and may not necessarily reflect the views of all stakeholders. This book is intended for awareness purpose towards environment and should not be considered as a definitive or authoritative source on the topics discussed. The authors assume no liability for any actions taken or decisions made based on the information contained within this book. This compilation of information is the result of extensive research, including insights gathered from lecture notes, internet resources, and academic discussions. We have strived to present relevant and essential content to empower readers with knowledge that can benefit humanity and foster a collective commitment to sustainable development. We express our deepest gratitude to the Almighty for granting us the strength and wisdom to complete this book. We also acknowledge the valuable contributions of all the resources that helped shape this work, including educators, researchers, and technology platforms. It is our sincere hope that this book serves as a guiding light for anyone striving to make a difference in the world.

Let us all work together towards achieving the SDGs, ensuring that our collective efforts pave the way for a sustainable and harmonious future.

Acknowledgement

We express our heartfelt gratitude to the Almighty for granting us the strength, wisdom, and perseverance to complete this book.This book is an effort by the authors to contribute to the benefit of society and the upliftment of mankind. It aims to create awareness about the Sustainable Development Goals, which are essential steps toward ensuring a better future for humanity.This book is a compilation of information gathered from various sources, including lecture notes, internet resources, and research materials. It is intended solely for societal awareness. By compiling relevant and necessary information, this work serves as a resource for understanding and promoting sustainability and humanity towards environment.Every effort has been made to ensure that the information compiled is accurate, relevant, and presented in a way that benefits readers.This book seeks to inspire individuals to work toward achieving these global goals for the betterment of mankind. This book is a reflection of collaborative knowledge and shared understanding, meant solely for societal awareness.We extend our gratitude to all the scholars, educators, and all the platforms whose contributions have indirectly enriched this work.Lastly, we thank everyone who has supported and encouraged me in this endeavor to make a meaningful contribution to humanity.

Disclaimer: This book presents information and perspectives gathered from various sources. While every effort has been made to ensure accuracy, the author does not claim that this book is entirely free from errors or omissions. The views and interpretations presented here are the author's own and may not necessarily reflect the views of all stakeholders. This book is intended for educational and informational purposes only and should not be considered as a definitive or authoritative source on the topics discussed. The author assumes no liability for any actions taken or decisions made based on the information contained within this book.

CONTENTS

No.	Topic Name	Page No.
Chapter 1	Introduction to the Sustainable Development Goals (SDGs)	(1-11)
1.1	Sustainable Development and SDGs	1
1.2	Analogy to understand the SDGs	1
1.3	Purpose of SDGs	3
1.4	Importance of Sustainable Development	6
Chapter 2	History and Evolution of the SDGs	(12-18)
2.1	From MDGs to SDGs	12
2.2	Addressing the Limitations of the MDGs	12
2.3	Key Milestones in the Development of SDGs	13
2.4	Main Challenges in Achieving the SDGs	14
Chapter 3	The 17 Sustainable Development Goals	(19-77)
3.1	Overview of the 17 Sustainable Development Goals	19
3.2	The 17 SDGs	19
3.3	Overview of Indicators Used to Measure Progress	49
Chapter 4	Empowerment and Future Scope of the SDGs	(78-101)
4.1	How to Contribute to Achieving the SDGs	78
4.2	The Role of People, Companies, and Governments	80
4.3	Working Together Locally and Globally	85
4.4	What's Next for the SDGs	87
4.5	New Ideas for a Sustainable Future	89
4.6	How Technology Can Help the SDGs	93
Chapter 5	SDGs and Industrial Revolutions	(102-105)
5.1	The First Industrial Revolution (IR 1.0)	102
5.2	The Second Industrial Revolution (IR 2.0)	103
5.3	The Third Industrial Revolution (IR 3.0)	103
5.4	The Fourth Industrial Revolution (IR 4.0)	104
5.5	The Fifth Industrial Revolution (IR 5.0)	104
5.6	The Sixth Industrial Revolution (IR 6.0)	104
5.7	The Seventh Industrial Revolution (IR 7.0)	105

Introduction to the Sustainable Development Goals (SDGs)

1.1Sustainable Development and SDGs

- **Sustainable development** means meeting our needs today without harming the ability of future generations to meet their own needs. It's about balancing our economic, social, and environmental needs to create a better life for all.

- The **Sustainable Development Goals (SDGs)** are a set of 17 global goals created by the United Nations in 2015. They aim to tackle the biggest challenges facing our world, such as poverty, inequality, climate change, and environmental degradation. The SDGs serve as a guide for countries and communities to work together towards a better future for everyone by the year 2030.

- The **Sustainable Development Goals (SDGs)** are thus as a collection of goals that are designed to make sure that everyone on our planet benefits from progress to improve life, not just a few people. They focus on reducing inequalities so that marginalized groups, like the poor or those facing discrimination, receive the help they need. Each goal focuses on different issues, such as ending poverty, ensuring quality education, promoting gender equality, and protecting the environment.This means that when countries work towards these goals, they aim to lift up everyone, ensuring no one is left behind.

1.2 Analogy to understand the SDGs

Imagine a community garden where everyone in the neighbourhood comes together to grow fruits and vegetables. Each person has a specific role, and they all work towards a common goal: to create a thriving garden that benefits everyone.

1. **No Poverty (SDG 1)**: Just like ensuring that everyone in the community has access to fresh produce, the goal is to eliminate poverty so that everyone can meet their basic needs.

2. **Zero Hunger (SDG 2)**: The garden provides food for all, ensuring that no one goes hungry. This goal aims to end hunger and ensure food security for everyone.

3. **Good Health and Well-Being (SDG 3)**: By growing healthy fruits and vegetables, the garden promotes better health for all community members, just as this goal focuses on improving health and well-being.
4. **Quality Education (SDG 4)**: The community can organize workshops in the garden to teach children and adults about gardening and nutrition, reflecting the importance of education for all.
5. **Gender Equality (SDG 5)**: In the garden, everyone has equal opportunities to contribute, regardless of gender. This goal emphasizes equal rights and opportunities for all people.
6. **Clean Water and Sanitation (SDG 6)**: The garden has a system for collecting rainwater and ensuring clean water is available for plants, similar to the goal of providing access to clean water and sanitation for everyone.
7. **Affordable and Clean Energy (SDG 7)**: If the garden uses solar lights to extend working hours, it represents the goal of promoting sustainable energy sources.
8. **Decent Work and Economic Growth (SDG 8)**: The garden can create jobs for local residents, helping boost the economy by providing work opportunities.
9. **Industry, Innovation, and Infrastructure (SDG 9)**: Building better tools or structures in the garden can improve productivity, just as this goal focuses on developing infrastructure and fostering innovation.
10. **Reduced Inequalities (SDG 10)**: The garden ensures that everyone has equal access to its resources, representing efforts to reduce inequalities within society.
11. **Sustainable Cities and Communities (SDG 11)**: A well-maintained garden contributes to a beautiful neighbourhood, promoting sustainable living in urban areas.
12. **Responsible Consumption and Production (SDG 12)**: The community practices composting and recycling waste from the garden, reflecting responsible consumption habits.
13. **Climate Action (SDG 13)**: By planting trees around the garden, the community helps combat climate change, similar to efforts aimed at protecting the environment.
14. **Life Below Water (SDG 14)**: If there's a pond in the garden that supports local wildlife, it highlights the importance of protecting aquatic ecosystems.

15. **Life on Land (SDG 15)**: The community takes care of the land by using sustainable gardening practices that preserve biodiversity.
16. **Peace, Justice, and Strong Institutions (SDG 16)**: The community works together peacefully to resolve conflicts about how to manage the garden, emphasizing cooperation and justice.
17. **Partnerships for the Goals (SDG 17)**: Finally, just as neighbors collaborate to make the garden successful, achieving the SDGs requires partnerships among governments, businesses, and communities worldwide.

This analogy illustrates how each SDG is interconnected like different aspects of maintaining a healthy community garden. Together, they contribute to creating a sustainable world where everyone can thrive.

1.3 Purpose of SDGs

The **purpose of these goals** is to create a world where all people can live healthy, fulfilling lives without harming the planet. The SDGs encourage everyone—governments, businesses, and individuals—to take action to make this vision a reality.

Objectives -The Sustainable Development Goals (SDG) - The main objectives of the Sustainable Development Goals (SDGs) are to promote sustainable growth, ensure well-being, economic growth, environmental legislation, and academic advancement. The SDGs aim to achieve a more equitable and just world through 17 goals detailing 169 targets, emphasizing the relevance of education in achieving these goals. These goals include ending poverty, reducing inequality, combating climate change, and building a sustainable futureofficially came into effect on January 1, 2016. **Table 1.1** outlines the unique aspects/objectives of each goal while highlighting their interconnections.

Table 1.1: SDG Insights: A comparative overview of focus areas and objectives.

SDG	Focus Area	Key Objectives	Similarities with Other SDGs	Unique Features
SDG 1: No Poverty	Eradication of poverty in all forms	Ensure access to basic services, reduce	Links to SDG 2 (hunger), SDG 3	Focus on income inequality and social

		vulnerability to disasters	(health), and SDG 8 (economic growth)	protection
SDG 2: Zero Hunger	End hunger, achieve food security, improve nutrition, sustainable agriculture	Double agricultural productivity, ensure food access, maintain genetic diversity	Links to SDG 1, SDG 3, and SDG 15 (life on land)	Specific focus on malnutrition and agricultural productivity
SDG 3: Good Health and Well-being	Ensure healthy lives and promote well-being	Reduce mortality, improve health systems, combat diseases	Links to SDG 6 (clean water) and SDG 2 (nutrition)	Emphasis on universal health coverage and global health threats like pandemics
SDG 4: Quality Education	Ensure inclusive and equitable education	Improve literacy and numeracy, provide lifelong learning opportunities	Links to SDG 5 (gender equality) and SDG 8	Focus on educational access for marginalized communities
SDG 5: Gender Equality	Achieve gender equality and empower women	End discrimination, violence, and harmful practices against women	Links to SDG 4 and SDG 10 (inequalities)	Emphasis on equal leadership opportunities and reproductive rights
SDG 6: Clean Water and Sanitation	Ensure water and sanitation for all	Improve water quality, reduce pollution, ensure sustainable water use	Links to SDG 3 and SDG 14 (life below water)	Focus on integrated water resource management
SDG 7: Affordable and Clean Energy	Ensure access to sustainable energy	Increase renewable energy, improve energy efficiency, expand access	Links to SDG 9 (industry) and SDG 13 (climate action)	Focus on renewable energy technologies and global energy access
SDG 8:	Promote	Achieve full	Links to	Focus on

Decent Work and Economic Growth	inclusive economic growth and decent work	employment, ensure safe workplaces, reduce youth unemployment	SDG 1, SDG 4, and SDG 9	sustained economic growth and global tourism
SDG 9: Industry, Innovation, and Infrastructure	Build resilient infrastructure, promote sustainable industrialization	Develop quality infrastructure, foster innovation, support small industries	Links to SDG 7, SDG 8, and SDG 11 (sustainable cities)	Focus on industrial growth and technological development
SDG 10: Reduced Inequalities	Reduce inequality within and among countries	Ensure equal opportunity, reduce income inequality, empower marginalized groups	Links to SDG 1 and SDG 5	Focus on policies for reducing income gaps within and among countries
SDG 11: Sustainable Cities and Communities	Make cities inclusive, safe, and sustainable	Improve urban planning, reduce environmental impacts, ensure access to housing	Links to SDG 9 and SDG 13	Emphasis on cultural heritage preservation and disaster resilience in urban areas
SDG 12: Responsible Consumption and Production	Ensure sustainable consumption and production patterns	Reduce waste, improve resource efficiency, promote sustainable practices	Links to SDG 6, SDG 7, and SDG 13	Focus on sustainable lifestyles and corporate responsibility
SDG 13: Climate Action	Combat climate change and its impacts	Strengthen climate resilience, integrate climate measures into policies	Links to SDG 7, SDG 14, and SDG 15	Emphasis on global cooperation for climate mitigation and adaptation
SDG 14: Life Below Water	Conserve and sustainably use oceans	Reduce marine pollution, protect ecosystems, regulate	Links to SDG 13 and SDG 15	Focus on marine biodiversity and the sustainable use of ocean

		fishing		resources
SDG 15: Life on Land	Protect, restore, and promote sustainable use of terrestrial ecosystems	Combat deforestation, desertification, halt biodiversity loss	Links to SDG 2 and SDG 13	Focus on protecting forest ecosystems and promoting sustainable land management
SDG 16: Peace, Justice, and Strong Institutions	Promote just, peaceful, and inclusive societies	Reduce violence, ensure access to justice, build accountable institutions	Links to SDG 10	Focus on anti-corruption measures and strong legal frameworks
SDG 17: Partnerships for the Goals	Strengthen global partnerships for sustainable development	Mobilize resources, enhance technology cooperation, build capacity	Links to all SDGs	Emphasis on global cooperation and partnerships

1.4 Importance of Sustainable Development

The Sustainable Development Goals (SDGs) aim to address multiple interconnected issues, such as poverty reduction and health improvement, by working on them simultaneously. They encourage global cooperation, as challenges like climate change affect everyone. The SDGs prioritize fairness and inclusion, ensuring all people, especially those disadvantaged, have access to opportunities and resources. Sustainable development also emphasizes long-term thinking, using resources wisely to ensure a healthy environment and quality of life for future generations. By addressing multiple issues simultaneously, the SDGs aim to create more effective solutions.

Sustainable development is important for several reasons:

1. **Global Cooperation**: The SDGs encourage countries to work together to solve problems that affect us all, like climate change and inequality.
2. **Interconnected Issues**: The goals are connected. For example, improving education (Goal 4) can help reduce poverty (Goal 1) because educated people often have better job opportunities.
3. **Focus on Everyone**: The SDGs aim to ensure that no one is left behind. This means helping the most vulnerable people in

society, such as those living in extreme poverty or facing discrimination.

Thus, the Sustainable Development Goals provide a clear plan for improving life on Earth while protecting our planet for future generations. They inspire everyone to take part in creating a fairer, healthier, and more sustainable world.

Simple Examples of Each Goals:

1. **No Poverty**: Helping families find jobs so they can support themselves.
2. **Zero Hunger**: Providing free meals to children in schools.
3. **Good Health and Well-Being**: Offering free health check-ups in communities.
4. **Quality Education**: Giving scholarships to students from low-income families.
5. **Gender Equality**: Ensuring women have the same job opportunities and pay as men.
6. **Clean Water and Sanitation**: Installing clean water wells in villages.
7. **Affordable and Clean Energy**: Using solar panels to provide electricity to homes.
8. **Decent Work and Economic Growth**: Supporting small businesses to create jobs.
9. **Industry, Innovation, and Infrastructure**: Building better roads and public transport systems.
10. **Reduced Inequalities**: Providing financial aid to help low-income families access healthcare.
11. **Sustainable Cities and Communities**: Creating parks that everyone can enjoy.
12. **Responsible Consumption and Production**: Encouraging recycling programs in neighbourhoods.
13. **Climate Action**: Organizing tree-planting events to combat climate change.
14. **Life Below Water**: Protecting marine areas from pollution and overfishing.
15. **Life on Land**: Restoring forests that have been cut down.
16. **Peace, Justice, and Strong Institutions**: Promoting community discussions about local governance.
17. **Partnerships for the Goals**: Encouraging businesses and governments to work together for sustainable development.

Everyone can play a role in achieving the SDGs by making small changes in their daily lives, such as reducing waste, supporting local businesses, or volunteering in their communities. By understanding the SDGs in this way, it becomes clear that they are not just abstract concepts but practical goals that can lead to positive changes for individuals and communities worldwide.**Table 1.2** includes simple, relatable examples that illustrate the real-world applications of each SDG.

Table 1.2: Examples that illustrate the real-world applications of each SDG.

SDG	Role in Addressing Global Challenges	Simple Examples
SDG 1: No Poverty	Reduces poverty and economic disparity by providing social protection and improving access to resources, enhancing resilience globally.	Helping families find jobs so they can support themselves.
SDG 2: Zero Hunger	Addresses food insecurity, malnutrition, and agricultural sustainability, ensuring equitable access to food for all.	Providing free meals to children in schools.
SDG 3: Good Health and Well-being	Tackles global health crises, reduces disease burden, and strengthens health systems for universal access to healthcare.	Offering free health check-ups in communities.
SDG 4: Quality Education	Equips individuals with knowledge and skills to overcome inequalities, reduce poverty, and foster innovation and sustainable growth.	Giving scholarships to students from low-income families.
SDG 5: Gender Equality	Eliminates gender disparities, promotes women's empowerment, and ensures equal opportunities to drive inclusive development.	Ensuring women have the same job opportunities and pay as men.
SDG 6: Clean Water and Sanitation	Ensures access to clean water and sanitation to combat water scarcity, pollution, and hygiene-related diseases.	Installing clean water wells in villages.
SDG 7: Affordable and Clean Energy	Accelerates global transition to clean energy, mitigating climate change and ensuring sustainable energy access for development.	Using solar panels to provide electricity to homes.
SDG 8: Decent	Promotes inclusive economic	Supporting small

Work and Economic Growth	growth, job creation, and fair laborpractices to reduce unemployment and foster sustainable economies.	businesses to create jobs.
SDG 9: Industry, Innovation, and Infrastructure	Supports industrial growth, resilient infrastructure, and technological innovation to address modern economic and social challenges.	Building better roads and public transport systems.
SDG 10: Reduced Inequalities	Reduces social and economic disparities within and between countries, ensuring equitable resource distribution and opportunities.	Providing financial aid to help low-income families access healthcare.
SDG 11: Sustainable Cities and Communities	Tackles urbanization challenges like housing, transportation, and environmental sustainability in cities worldwide.	Creating parks that everyone can enjoy.
SDG 12: Responsible Consumption and Production	Promotes sustainable resource use, waste reduction, and environmentally friendly practices to combat resource depletion.	Encouraging recycling programs in neighborhoods.
SDG 13: Climate Action	Mitigates and adapts to climate change by fostering global cooperation and implementing resilient strategies.	Organizing tree-planting events to combat climate change.
SDG 14: Life Below Water	Conserves marine ecosystems, combats ocean pollution, and ensures the sustainable use of aquatic resources.	Protecting marine areas from pollution and overfishing.
SDG 15: Life on Land	Protects terrestrial ecosystems, combats deforestation, and restores biodiversity to maintain environmental stability.	Restoring forests that have been cut down.
SDG 16: Peace, Justice, and Strong Institutions	Promotes peace, reduces violence, and strengthens institutions to address governance and conflict-related challenges.	Promoting community discussions about local governance.
SDG 17: Partnerships for the Goals	Encourages global collaboration, resource mobilization, and knowledge sharing to tackle global challenges collectively.	Encouraging businesses and governments to work together for sustainable development.

Chapter Highlights

The SDGs are 17 global goals created by the United Nations in 2015 to address global challenges like poverty, inequality, climate change, and environmental degradation.

- The SDGs aim to ensure everyone benefits from progress to improve life, not just a few people.
- Goals focus on reducing inequalities, promoting gender equality, and protecting the environment.
- The SDGs are interconnected and aim to create a sustainable world where everyone can thrive.
- Key objectives include no poverty, zero hunger, good health and well-being, quality education, gender equality, clean water and sanitation, affordable and clean energy, decent work and economic growth, industry, innovation, and infrastructure, reduced inequalities, sustainable cities and communities, responsible consumption and production, climate action, life below water, life on land, peace, justice, and strong institutions, and partnerships for the goals.
- SDG 1 focuses on eliminating poverty, ensuring access to basic services, and reducing vulnerability to disasters.
- SDGs 2 (hunger), SDG 3 (health), and SDG 8 (economic growth) address income inequality and social protection.
- SDG 4 focuses on quality education, ensuring inclusive and equitable education, gender equality, clean water and sanitation, affordable and clean energy, decent work and economic growth, sustainable cities and communities, responsible consumption and production, climate action, life below water, life on land, peace, justice, and strong institutions.
- SDG 5 focuses on gender equality and empower women, achieving gender equality and empowering marginalized groups.
- SDG 6 focuses on clean water and sanitation, ensuring water quality, reducing pollution, and sustainable water use.
- SDG 7 focuses on affordable and clean energy, sustainable cities and communities, and climate action.
- SDG 11 focuses on sustainable cities and communities, promoting inclusive, safe, and sustainable urban planning,

cultural heritage preservation, and disaster resilience in urban areas.

- The SDGs are important for global cooperation, interconnected issues, and focusing on everyone.
- Individuals can play a role in achieving the SDGs by making small changes in their daily lives, such as reducing waste, supporting local businesses, or volunteering in their communities.

2.1 From MDGs to SDGs

Before the SDGs, there were the **Millennium Development Goals (MDGs)**. The MDGs were eight goals set by the United Nations in 2000 to address extreme poverty, hunger, and disease. While the MDGs made some progress, they had limitations. The SDGs were developed/created to build on the MDGs and address a broader range of issues.

2.2 Addressing the Limitations of the MDGs

The **Sustainable Development Goals (SDGs)** were created to fix some of the problems with the **Millennium Development Goals (MDGs)**. Here's how they improved things:

- **Broader Focus:** The MDGs mainly looked at social issues like poverty and health. In contrast, the SDGs cover a much wider range of topics, including economic growth (how countries can make money), protecting the environment, and ensuring everyone is included in progress. This means they recognize that these issues are all connected.

- **Fairness for All:** The SDGs focus on reducing inequalities both within countries and between them. They aim to make sure that everyone benefits from progress, especially those who are often left behind, like marginalized communities. The MDGs didn't always pay attention to these differences in how people were doing.

- **Local Solutions:** The SDGs encourage countries to adapt their goals to fit their specific situations instead of following a strict global plan. This flexibility allows each country to develop strategies that work best for them based on their unique challenges and needs.

- **Comprehensive Goals:** The SDGs have 169 specific targets that cover many aspects of development. This holistic approach means they look at the bigger picture rather than just focusing on one issue at a time. In contrast, the MDGs had fewer goals, which sometimes meant important problems were overlooked.

In summary, the SDGs aim to create a more inclusive, fair, and comprehensive approach to global development compared to the MDGs.

2.3 Key Milestones in the Development of SDGs

In 2014, the **Open Working Group** proposed 17 goals and 169 targets for the Sustainable Development Goals (SDGs). The SDGs officially came into effect in 2016.

The **Open Working Group (OWG)** was established by the UN General Assembly in 2013 to develop recommendations for the SDGs. It played a crucial role by:

- **Drafting Goals**: The OWG proposed 17 goals and 169 targets after extensive consultations with various stakeholders, ensuring diverse perspectives were considered in goal formulation.
- **Building Consensus**: By involving representatives from different countries and sectors, the OWG helped build consensus around sustainable development priorities that reflect global needs while accommodating local contexts.

Following are some important events / key milestones that led to the development/creation of SDGs:

- 2012: The United Nations Conference on Sustainable Development (Rio+20 conference) took place in Brazil, where countries agreed to create a new set of goals.
- 2013: The UN General Assembly established an Open Working Group to develop the SDGs.
- 2014: The Open Working Group proposed 17 goals and 169 targets.
- 2015: The UN General Assembly adopted the 17 SDGs and their targets.
- 2016: The SDGs officially came into effect, and countries began working towards achieving them by 2030.

Some examples of targets in the SDGs include:

- Ending poverty in all its forms everywhere.
- Ensuring everyone has access to quality education.
- Achieving gender equality and empowering all women and girls.
- Promoting sustainable economic growth and decent work for all.
- Taking urgent action to combat climate change and its impacts.

2.4 Main Challenges in Achieving the SDGs

Achieving the **Sustainable Development Goals (SDGs)** is not easy, and there are several big challenges. Here's a simple breakdown of the main issues:

Inequality: Inequality is a major problem. This means that some people have a lot more money and opportunities than others. Many people still lack access to education, healthcare, and basic needs because of their gender, race, or where they live. To make real progress on the SDGs, we need to tackle these inequalities.

- **Resource Scarcity:** Many developing countries don't have enough resources—like money or materials—to achieve the SDGs. There's a huge gap between what is needed (about $4 trillion each year) and what is currently available. Poor communities often live in areas that need urgent help, but they don't always get the funding they need.

- **Political Hurdles:** Political issues can slow down progress. If governments are unstable or don't care about international agreements, it can lead to little action being taken. Additionally, when big companies avoid paying taxes, it reduces the money that governments have to spend on projects related to the SDGs.

- **Global Crises:** Current global problems like climate change, the COVID-19 pandemic, and conflicts (such as the war in Ukraine) have made it harder to achieve the SDGs. These crises hit vulnerable communities the hardest and make existing inequalities worse, making it difficult to reach the goals by 2030.

- **Lack of Collaboration:** To achieve the SDGs, different groups—like governments, businesses, and international organizations—need to work together. However, there is often a lack of teamwork and coordination among these groups, which can prevent effective action.

- **Fiscal Constraints:** Many governments are facing budget cuts that limit their ability to invest in important areas like education and healthcare. This focus on cutting costs can stop necessary investments that are crucial for achieving the SDGs.

To overcome these challenges, everyone—governments, businesses, and communities—needs to work together to ensure that progress towards the SDGs is fair and sustainable for all people.**Table**

2.1summarizes the importance of each Sustainable Development Goal (SDG) and the main challenges in achieving them

Table 2.1: Challenges and Significance of the Sustainable Development Goals.

SDG	Importance	Main Challenges
SDG 1: No Poverty	Eliminates extreme poverty, enhances quality of life, and ensures access to basic services.	Economic inequality, lack of social protection, political instability, and limited financial resources.
SDG 2: Zero Hunger	Ensures food security, combats malnutrition, and promotes sustainable agriculture.	Climate change, food distribution inefficiencies, soil degradation, and conflicts disrupting food systems.
SDG 3: Good Health and Well-being	Promotes healthy lives, reduces global disease burden, and improves healthcare systems.	Limited access to healthcare, pandemic outbreaks, high healthcare costs, and health inequities.
SDG 4: Quality Education	Provides equal opportunities for learning and improves social and economic mobility.	Inadequate funding, gender inequality, lack of qualified teachers, and digital divide in education access.
SDG 5: Gender Equality	Empowers women, reduces discrimination, and ensures equal opportunities for all genders.	Deeply rooted cultural norms, gender-based violence, and underrepresentation of women in decision-making.
SDG 6: Clean Water and Sanitation	Ensures access to safe water, improves sanitation, and reduces waterborne diseases.	Water scarcity, pollution, poor infrastructure, and lack of integrated water management systems.
SDG 7: Affordable and	Promotes renewable energy, reduces	High initial costs of clean energy, lack of

Clean Energy	environmental impact, and enhances energy efficiency.	infrastructure, and dependency on fossil fuels.
SDG 8: Decent Work and Economic Growth	Creates jobs, promotes sustainable economic growth, and ensures fair labor standards.	High unemployment, unsafe working conditions, economic disparities, and automation displacing jobs.
SDG 9: Industry, Innovation, and Infrastructure	Strengthens infrastructure, fosters innovation, and supports industrial growth.	Limited technological access, lack of funding, and uneven industrialization in developing regions.
SDG 10: Reduced Inequalities	Promotes social inclusion, equal opportunities, and fair economic distribution.	Institutionalized discrimination, income inequality, and lack of equitable policies.
SDG 11: Sustainable Cities and Communities	Creates safe, resilient, and sustainable urban environments.	Rapid urbanization, housing shortages, inadequate infrastructure, and environmental degradation.
SDG 12: Responsible Consumption and Production	Promotes sustainable practices and reduces waste.	Consumer habits, industrial inefficiencies, and insufficient implementation of recycling systems.
SDG 13: Climate Action	Mitigates climate change impacts and promotes global cooperation.	Political resistance, lack of funding, inadequate climate policies, and slow adoption of renewable energy.
SDG 14: Life Below Water	Protects marine ecosystems, ensures sustainable fisheries, and reduces ocean pollution.	Overfishing, plastic pollution, climate change-induced ocean warming, and weak marine protection policies.
SDG 15: Life on Land	Conserves terrestrial ecosystems, combats	Illegal logging, urban sprawl, land degradation,

	deforestation, and restores biodiversity.	and lack of global coordination for biodiversity protection.
SDG 16: Peace, Justice, and Strong Institutions	Promotes just societies, reduces violence, and strengthens governance.	Corruption, weak institutions, conflict zones, and lack of access to justice systems.
SDG 17: Partnerships for the Goals	Strengthens global cooperation and mobilizes resources for sustainable development.	Political differences, insufficient funding, and lack of collaboration between governments and stakeholders.

Chapter Highlights

- The SDGs were developed to address the limitations of the Millennium Development Goals (MDGs), which were eight goals set by the United Nations in 2000.
- The SDGs focus on economic growth, environmental protection, and inclusion for everyone, reducing inequalities within and between countries.
- The SDGs have 169 specific targets covering many aspects of development, providing a more inclusive, fair, and comprehensive approach to global development.
- Key milestones in the development of the SDGs include the establishment of the Open Working Group (OWG) in 2013 and the 2012 United Nations Conference on Sustainable Development (Rio+20 conference).
- The SDGs have targets including ending poverty, ensuring access to quality education, achieving gender equality, promoting sustainable economic growth, and taking urgent action to combat climate change.
- Achieving the SDGs is challenging due to inequality, resource scarcity, political hurdles, global crises, lack of collaboration, and financial constraints.
- Inequality is a major issue, with many people still lacking access to education, healthcare, and basic needs due to their gender, race, or location.

- Political hurdles can slow down progress, and current global problems like climate change, the COVID-19 pandemic, and conflicts like the war in Ukraine have made it harder to achieve the SDGs.
- Collaboration among different groups is essential for achieving the SDGs, but often lacks teamwork and coordination.
- To overcome these challenges, everyone—governments, businesses, and communities—needs to work together to ensure fair and sustainable progress towards the SDGs.

Chapter 3

The 17 Sustainable Development Goals

3.1 Overview of the 17 Sustainable Development Goals

The 17 Sustainable Development Goals (SDGs), established by the United Nations, are a global set of ambitions aiming to address critical issues like poverty, hunger, health, education, climate change, gender equality, and environmental sustainability by 2030, with a focus on achieving "peace, prosperity for people and the planet" through collaborative action by all nations, ensuring "no one is left behind.

3.2 The 17 SDGs

The SDGs were developed through an inclusive and transparent process involving governments, civil society, the private sector, and international organizations. The process began in 2012, with the UN Conference on Sustainable Development (Rio+20), which mandated the creation of a set of sustainable development goals. Over the next three years, the UN Open Working Group on Sustainable Development Goals, comprising 30 countries, drafted the goals and targets.

1. **No Poverty**: Eradicate extreme poverty and ensure social protection for all.
2. **Zero Hunger**: End hunger and ensure access to nutritious food for all.
3. **Good Health and Well-being**: Ensure healthy lives and promote well-being for all.
4. **Quality Education**: Provide inclusive and equitable quality education for all.
5. **Gender Equality**: Achieve gender equality and empower all women and girls.
6. **Clean Water and Sanitation**: Ensure access to clean water and sanitation for all.
7. **Affordable and Clean Energy**: Ensure access to affordable and clean energy for all.
8. **Decent Work and Economic Growth**: Promote sustained economic growth and decent work for all.
9. **Industry, Innovation, and Infrastructure**: Build resilient infrastructure and promote sustainable industrialization.
10. **Reduced Inequalities**: Reduce inequalities within and among countries.

11. **Sustainable Cities and Communities**: Build sustainable and resilient cities and communities.
12. **Responsible Consumption and Production**: Ensure sustainable consumption and production patterns.
13. **Climate Action**: Take urgent action to combat climate change.
14. **Life Below Water**: Conserve and sustainably use oceans, seas, and marine resources.
15. **Life on Land**: Protect, restore, and promote sustainable use of ecosystems.
16. **Peace, Justice, and Strong Institutions**: Promote peace, justice, and strong institutions.
17. **Partnerships for the Goals**: Strengthen global partnerships for sustainable development.

Key Features

- **Integrated and Interconnected**: The SDGs recognize the interconnectedness of economic, social, and environmental challenges.

- **Universal**: The SDGs apply to all countries, regardless of income level or development status.

- **Ambitious**: The SDGs set specific, measurable targets for 2030.

- **Indicators**: Each goal has a set of indicators to track progress.

Implementation and Progress

- **National Implementation**: Countries are responsible for implementing the SDGs through national plans and policies.

- **Global Monitoring**: The UN tracks progress through the Sustainable Development Goals Report.

- **Voluntary National Reviews**: Countries submit voluntary reviews of their progress.

Challenges and Opportunities

- **Financing**: Achieving the SDGs requires significant investment.

- **Climate Change**: Climate change poses a significant threat to SDG progress.

- **Inequality**: Persistent inequalities hinder SDG progress.

- **Technology**: Technology can accelerate SDG progress.

- **Partnerships**: Collaboration among governments, civil society, and the private sector is crucial.

The SDGs offer a unique opportunity for countries to work together to address the world's most pressing challenges and create a better future for all.

Table 3.1 UN SDGs: Goals, targets, and indicators.

Goal No.	Goal Name	Description	Key Targets	Progress Indicators	Challenges and Opportunities
1	No Poverty	Eradicate extreme poverty and ensure social protection for all.	Eradicate extreme poverty, reduce poverty, implement social protection	Percentage of population living below international poverty line, social protection coverage	Inequality, lack of access to education and job opportunities
2	Zero Hunger	End hunger and ensure access to nutritious food for all.	End hunger, achieve food security, improve nutrition	Prevalence of undernourishment, prevalence of stunting	Climate change, conflict, lack of agricultural infrastructure
3	Good Health and Well-being	Ensure healthy lives and promote well-being for all.	Reduce maternal mortality, end epidemics, ensure universal health coverage	Maternal mortality ratio, life expectancy at birth, health insurance coverage	Inadequate healthcare infrastructure, lack of healthcare professionals
4	Quality Education	Provide inclusive and equitable quality education for all.	Ensure universal primary education, increase access to higher education, improve	Out-of-school children, literacy rate, pupil-teacher ratio	Lack of access to education, inadequate education infrastructure

			education quality		
5	Gender Equality	Achieve gender equality and empower all women and girls.	End discrimination, eliminate violence, ensure participation and leadership	Percentage of women in parliament, percentage of women in labor force	Discrimination, violence, lack of access to education and job opportunities
6	Clean Water and Sanitation	Ensure access to clean water and sanitation for all.	Universal access to safe drinking water, sanitation and hygiene	Percentage of population using safely managed drinking water, percentage of population using safely managed sanitation	Lack of access to clean water and sanitation, inadequate infrastructure
7	Affordable and Clean Energy	Ensure access to affordable and clean energy for all.	Increase access to energy, improve energy efficiency, increase share of renewable energy	Access to electricity, renewable energy share in the energy mix	Lack of access to energy, inadequate energy infrastructure
8	Decent Work and Economic Growth	Promote sustained economic growth and decent work for all.	Achieve higher levels of economic productivity, promote entrepreneurship, improve working conditions	GDP growth rate, unemployment rate, labor productivity	Inequality, lack of access to education and job opportunities
9	Industry, Innovation, and Infrastructure	Build resilient infrastructure and promote sustainable industrialization.	Develop sustainable infrastructure, promote inclusive and sustainable industrializa	Investment in infrastructure, manufacturing value added	Lack of access to infrastructure, inadequate industrial infrastructure

			tion		
10	Reduced Inequalities	Reduce inequalities within and among countries.	Reduce income inequalities, promote social inclusion, reduce inequality within and among countries	Income inequality, social protection coverage	Inequality, lack of access to education and job opportunities
11	Sustainable Cities and Communities	Build sustainable and resilient cities and communities.	Ensure access to safe and affordable housing, improve urban planning, reduce urban pollution	Urban population living in slums, municipal waste management	Lack of access to safe and affordable housing, inadequate urban infrastructure
12	Responsible Consumption and Production	Ensure sustainable consumption and production patterns.	Implement sustainable consumption and production, reduce waste, increase resource efficiency	Material footprint, domestic material consumption	Unsustainable consumption patterns, lack of resource efficiency
13	Climate Action	Take urgent action to combat climate change.	Strengthen resilience, promote climate-resilient agriculture, integrate climate change measures	Greenhouse gas emissions, climate change adaptation and mitigation	Climate change, lack of climate resilience
14	Life Below Water	Conserve and sustainably use oceans, seas, and marine resources.	Reduce marine pollution, protect marine ecosystems, promote	Marine protected areas, fish stocks within biologically sustainable levels	Marine pollution, overfishing

			sustainable fishing	
15	Life on Land	Protect, restore, and promote sustainable use of ecosystems.	Conserve and restore ecosystems, promote sustainable forest management, combat desertification	Forest area, proportion of terrestrial ecosystem under protection	Deforestation, land degradation
16	Peace, Justice, and Strong Institutions	Promote peace, justice, and strong institutions.	Reduce violence, promote rule of law, ensure inclusive and participatory decision-making	Homicide rate, prisoners held without sentencing, bribery incidence	Conflict, corruption, lack of access to justice
17	Partnerships for the Goals	Strengthen global partnerships for sustainable development.	Finance and technology transfer, capacity-building, systemic issues	Official development assistance, technology transfer,	

3.2.1 Goal 1: No Poverty – End Poverty in All Its Forms Everywhere

Goal 1 of the United Nations Sustainable Development Goals (SDGs) focuses on eradicating poverty in all its forms by 2030. This goal seeks to ensure that every individual, regardless of where they live, has access to the resources and opportunities needed to live a dignified life.

Key Objectives:

1. **Eradicate Extreme Poverty:** The primary aim of Goal 1 is to end extreme poverty, which is defined as living on less than $1.90 a day. The goal emphasizes addressing the root causes of poverty, such as unemployment, lack of education, inequality, and limited access to basic services.

2. **Reduce the Proportion of People Living in Poverty:** In addition to eliminating extreme poverty, Goal 1 aims to reduce the percentage of people living below national poverty lines.

This involves creating economic opportunities, improving social safety nets, and increasing access to essential services like healthcare and education.

3. **Ensure Equal Access to Resources:** Goal 1 advocates for ensuring that all individuals, especially marginalized groups such as women, children, the elderly, and people with disabilities, have equal access to economic resources, social services, and opportunities. This includes improving access to education, employment, and financial services.

4. **Access to Basic Services and Resources:** Access to food, clean water, healthcare, shelter, and education is essential to reducing poverty. Goal 1 focuses on ensuring that these basic needs are met for all people, regardless of income level or geographic location.

5. **Promote Inclusive and Sustainable Economic Growth:** Achieving sustainable development requires creating job opportunities and promoting inclusive economic growth. Goal 1 calls for the creation of long-term, inclusive economic growth that helps lift people out of poverty and ensures they have opportunities to improve their quality of life.

6. **Address Vulnerable Populations:** Special focus is given to the most vulnerable populations, such as those living in conflict zones, rural areas, and informal settlements. These groups are often disproportionately affected by poverty and are at higher risk of being left behind in development efforts.

7. **Expand Social Protection Systems:** Social protection systems, such as unemployment benefits, child support, pensions, and healthcare, are crucial in preventing people from falling deeper into poverty. Goal 1 emphasizes expanding and strengthening social safety nets to help those in need and reduce inequalities.

8. **Promote Equal Opportunities for All:** To end poverty, it's essential to address inequality and ensure that everyone has an equal chance to succeed. This includes providing equal access to education, healthcare, and employment opportunities for all individuals, regardless of gender, ethnicity, or social background.

Why Goal 1 Matters:

Poverty is a significant barrier to development and well-being. It affects access to education, healthcare, and basic necessities, and leads to cycles of inequality and deprivation. By eradicating poverty, we can create a foundation for achieving other SDGs, such as improving health, education, and economic growth.

Goal 1 matters because it is fundamental to the overall success of sustainable development. If poverty is not addressed, it undermines efforts to achieve all other goals, including gender equality, climate action, and sustainable economic development. Ending poverty is essential for creating a fair, just, and sustainable world where everyone has the opportunity to thrive.

3.2.2 Goal 2: Zero Hunger – End Hunger and Ensure Food Security for All

Goal 2 of the United Nations Sustainable Development Goals (SDGs) aims to end hunger, achieve food security, and improve nutrition by 2030. It focuses on ensuring that everyone, everywhere, has access to enough nutritious food to lead healthy lives.

Key Objectives:

1. **End Hunger Worldwide:** The primary aim is to make sure no one goes hungry by providing enough food for everyone, especially the most vulnerable people in poverty-stricken or disaster-affected areas.

2. **Improve Nutrition:** Focus is placed on ensuring that people not only have enough to eat but also have access to nutritious and balanced diets, particularly for children, pregnant women, and other vulnerable groups.

3. **Support Sustainable Agriculture:** This goal promotes farming methods that produce more food while protecting the environment, using fewer resources, and adapting to climate change.

4. **Help Small-Scale Farmers:** Special support is given to small and family farmers by improving their access to resources like seeds, technology, and markets, so they can grow more food and earn better incomes.

5. **Strengthen Food Systems:** Building strong food supply systems ensures that food is available, accessible, and affordable, even during emergencies like droughts or conflicts.

6. **Reduce Food Waste:** Minimizing food loss during production and cutting food waste in homes and stores are essential to ensuring enough food for everyone.

Why Goal 2 Matters:

Hunger affects billions of people, causing malnutrition, poor health, and reduced productivity. Children who are hungry cannot grow, learn, or thrive. By achieving zero hunger, we can improve lives, boost economies, and build healthier, more resilient communities.

Achieving Goal 2 requires the joint efforts of governments, farmers, businesses, and individuals to create a world where everyone has enough nutritious food to eat, leaving no one behind.

3.2.3 Goal 3: Good Health and Well-Being – Ensure Healthy Lives and Promote Well-Being for All

Goal 3 of the United Nations Sustainable Development Goals (SDGs) focuses on ensuring that everyone, regardless of age or location, can live a healthy life. It aims to improve overall well-being and reduce the global burden of diseases and preventable deaths by 2030.

Key Objectives:

1. **Reduce Preventable Deaths:** The goal aims to significantly lower deaths caused by diseases, such as malaria, HIV/AIDS, tuberculosis, and non-communicable diseases like diabetes, cancer, and heart conditions. It also seeks to end preventable deaths of newborns and children under 5 years old.

2. **Improve Maternal Health:** Special emphasis is placed on reducing deaths during pregnancy and childbirth by ensuring access to quality maternal healthcare services.

3. **Combat Epidemics:** Efforts focus on preventing and managing outbreaks of infectious diseases, including pandemics, by strengthening healthcare systems and promoting vaccination programs.

4. **Ensure Universal Healthcare:** Goal 3 emphasizes access to affordable, quality healthcare services, including medicines and vaccines, for everyone, especially those in low-income communities.

5. **Promote Mental Health:** Addressing mental health issues and preventing substance abuse are critical parts of this goal, aiming to reduce suicides and improve overall mental well-being.

6. **Strengthen Healthcare Systems:** Building resilient healthcare systems, increasing healthcare funding, and ensuring the availability of trained healthcare workers are essential for achieving this goal.

7. **Address Environmental Health Risks:** Reducing deaths and illnesses caused by pollution, unsafe water, and hazardous chemicals is also a priority to improve public health.

Why Goal 3 Matters:

Good health is essential for individuals to live fulfilling lives, contribute to their communities, and drive economic growth. Poor health and lack of access to healthcare can trap families in poverty, reduce productivity, and strain public resources.

Achieving Goal 3 requires a global commitment to improving healthcare access, funding research, and ensuring that no one is left behind, creating a healthier and more equitable world for all.

3.2.4 Goal 4: Quality Education – Ensure Inclusive and Equitable Quality Education and Promote Lifelong Learning Opportunities for All

Goal 4 of the United Nations Sustainable Development Goals (SDGs) is focused on ensuring that everyone has access to high-quality education, regardless of their background, gender, or location. It aims to provide opportunities for learning throughout life to help individuals thrive in a rapidly changing world.

Key Objectives:

1. **Ensure Free and Quality Education for All:** The goal aims to provide free, high-quality primary and secondary education for all children, regardless of their socioeconomic status. This includes ensuring that education is accessible and inclusive for marginalized groups, such as girls, children with disabilities, and those in conflict areas.

2. **Promote Early Childhood Development:** Special attention is given to early childhood education, focusing on ensuring that all children have access to good-quality pre-primary education that lays the foundation for future learning.

3. **Access to Higher Education:** The goal advocates for increasing access to affordable higher education, including vocational and technical training, to help people gain the skills needed for employment and personal growth.

4. **Promote Skills for Work and Lifelong Learning:** Education is not only about academic knowledge but also about building skills for work and life. This includes promoting vocational education and lifelong learning opportunities to help individuals adapt to changing job markets.

5. **Achieve Gender Equality in Education:** Ensuring equal access to education for boys and girls is essential, particularly for eliminating gender disparities in school enrollment, retention, and graduation rates.

6. **Improve Education Quality and Teacher Training:** Goal 4 emphasizes improving the quality of education through better teacher training, curriculum development, and learning resources. This includes ensuring that schools have the necessary infrastructure and tools to provide effective learning experiences.

7. **Increase Education for Sustainable Development:** This goal promotes education that encourages sustainable lifestyles, environmental awareness, and social responsibility, empowering students to become active global citizens.

Why Goal 4 Matters:

Education is a powerful tool for reducing poverty, improving health, and promoting equality. It empowers individuals to break the cycle of poverty, gain better job opportunities, and contribute to economic development. Quality education also fosters innovation, social cohesion, and sustainable development.

Achieving Goal 4 requires global efforts from governments, educators, communities, and individuals to ensure that education is accessible, inclusive, and of high quality for everyone, promoting lifelong learning and creating opportunities for a better future.

3.2.5 Goal 5: Gender Equality – Achieve Gender Equality and Empower All Women and Girls

Goal 5 of the United Nations Sustainable Development Goals (SDGs) focuses on achieving gender equality and empowering all women and girls. It aims to end discrimination, violence, and harmful practices based on gender, ensuring that women and girls have equal opportunities to thrive and contribute to society.

Key Objectives:

1. **End Discrimination:** Goal 5 aims to eliminate all forms of discrimination against women and girls, including in laws, policies, and practices, ensuring that they are treated equally in all aspects of life.

2. **End Violence and Harmful Practices:** This goal seeks to end violence against women and girls, such as domestic violence,

sexual harassment, trafficking, and harmful traditional practices like child marriage and female genital mutilation.

3. **Ensure Equal Participation in Leadership:** Goal 5 promotes equal participation of women and girls in decision-making processes, political leadership, and all levels of governance, encouraging their involvement in shaping policies and solutions.

4. **Ensure Equal Access to Education and Health:** Ensuring that women and girls have equal access to quality education, healthcare, and economic opportunities is a critical part of this goal. This includes addressing barriers such as child marriage, early pregnancies, and lack of access to reproductive health services.

5. **Promote Equal Economic Opportunities:** Goal 5 aims to ensure that women and girls have equal access to economic resources

3.2.6 Goal 6: Clean Water and Sanitation – Ensure Availability and Sustainable Management of Water and Sanitation for All

Goal 6 of the United Nations Sustainable Development Goals (SDGs) focuses on ensuring access to clean water and sanitation for everyone, while promoting sustainable management of water resources. It aims to address water scarcity, improve water quality, and ensure safe sanitation for all people, regardless of where they live.

Key Objectives:

1. **Universal Access to Safe Water:** The goal aims to ensure that all people have access to clean and safe drinking water, free from contamination. This includes improving water infrastructure and making water available in rural and underserved communities.

2. **Improved Sanitation and Hygiene:** Goal 6 promotes the provision of access to adequate sanitation facilities, including toilets and sewage systems, to reduce open defecation and improve hygiene practices, which are essential for preventing disease.

3. **Reduce Water Pollution:** Efforts are focused on reducing pollution in water bodies by cutting down on the release of harmful chemicals and waste, which can degrade water quality and harm ecosystems and human health.

4. **Improve Water Efficiency:** The goal promotes the efficient use of water in agriculture, industry, and domestic settings, encouraging water-saving practices and technologies to reduce waste.

5. **Protect and Restore Water Ecosystems:** Goal 6 calls for the protection and restoration of water ecosystems, such as rivers, lakes, and wetlands, which are vital for maintaining clean water sources, biodiversity, and climate resilience.

6. **Increase International Cooperation:** The goal encourages collaboration between countries to manage transboundary water resources, ensuring that water is shared equitably and used sustainably across borders.

7. **Support Water-Related Education and Awareness:** Raising awareness about water conservation, sanitation, and hygiene practices is crucial for creating a culture of sustainability and promoting responsible water use among communities.

Why Goal 6 Matters:

Access to clean water and sanitation is fundamental to health, well-being, and sustainable development. Without it, communities suffer from waterborne diseases, lack of hygiene, and environmental degradation. Achieving Goal 6 ensures that everyone can live in healthier environments, enjoy better quality of life, and contribute to economic growth.

Achieving Goal 6 requires collective action from governments, communities, and individuals to protect water resources, improve sanitation, and ensure sustainable access for all, leaving no one behind.

3.2.7 Goal 7: Affordable and Clean Energy – Ensure Access to Affordable, Reliable, Sustainable, and Modern Energy for All

Goal 7 of the United Nations Sustainable Development Goals (SDGs) aims to ensure that everyone has access to affordable, reliable, and clean energy. It focuses on increasing the use of renewable energy sources, improving energy efficiency, and making energy accessible to all, especially in underserved communities.

Key Objectives:

1. **Universal Access to Modern Energy:** The goal seeks to ensure that everyone, everywhere, has access to affordable and reliable energy services, including electricity and clean cooking solutions, which are essential for improving quality of life and supporting economic development.

2. **Increase Renewable Energy Use:** Goal 7 emphasizes the transition to renewable energy sources such as solar, wind, hydro, and geothermal power. This is essential for reducing dependency on fossil fuels, mitigating climate change, and ensuring long-term energy security.

3. **Improve Energy Efficiency:** The goal aims to improve energy efficiency in all sectors, including industry, transportation, and residential areas. By using energy more effectively, we can reduce waste, lower energy costs, and decrease greenhouse gas emissions.

4. **Promote Research and Innovation:** Encouraging investment in research, development, and innovation in energy technologies is crucial for finding new, more sustainable ways to produce and use energy.

5. **Support Energy Infrastructure:** Goal 7 focuses on developing energy infrastructure and technology that ensures access to energy in rural and remote areas, addressing the energy access gap that exists in many parts of the world.

6. **Foster International Cooperation:** The goal promotes collaboration between countries to share knowledge, technologies, and funding to support energy projects, especially in developing nations, and to help them transition to cleaner energy sources.

Why Goal 7 Matters:

Energy is a key driver of economic growth, social development, and environmental sustainability. Lack of access to clean and affordable energy can hinder progress in education, health, and industry. By ensuring access to modern energy for all, Goal 7 aims to improve lives, reduce poverty, and protect the planet.

Achieving Goal 7 requires a global effort to scale up clean energy technologies, improve energy access, and promote energy-efficient practices, making energy more accessible, affordable, and sustainable for all.

3.2.8 Goal 8: Decent Work and Economic Growth – Promote Sustained, Inclusive, and Sustainable Economic Growth, Full and Productive Employment, and Decent Work for All

Goal 8 of the United Nations Sustainable Development Goals (SDGs) focuses on promoting inclusive and sustainable economic growth, as well as ensuring that everyone has access to decent work opportunities.

It aims to foster economic development that provides equal opportunities, reduces inequality, and creates jobs for all people, especially in developing countries.

Key Objectives:

1. **Promote Economic Growth:** Goal 8 seeks to promote sustained and inclusive economic growth, focusing on raising living standards and improving economic opportunities for all people, regardless of their background or location.

2. **Achieve Full and Productive Employment:** The goal aims to ensure that everyone has access to full and productive employment, where they are fairly compensated and have the opportunity to use their skills to their full potential. This includes promoting job creation and reducing unemployment.

3. **Ensure Decent Work for All:** The goal emphasizes providing decent work conditions, including safe working environments, fair wages, and rights for workers, such as freedom of association and protection from exploitation.

4. **Promote Entrepreneurship and Innovation:** Goal 8 encourages the development of new businesses, innovation, and the creation of job opportunities, particularly for youth, women, and marginalized groups.

5. **Increase Economic Productivity:** The goal focuses on improving productivity through technological innovation, skill development, and investment in sustainable industries, ensuring that economic growth leads to long-term prosperity.

6. **Reduce Youth Unemployment:** Special attention is given to reducing youth unemployment by improving access to education, vocational training, and apprenticeships, enabling young people to gain the skills needed for the job market.

7. **Promote Sustainable Tourism and Industry:** Goal 8 encourages industries and businesses to adopt sustainable practices that are both economically and environmentally viable, contributing to long-term growth while protecting resources for future generations.

8. **Address Informal and Precarious Work:** The goal also seeks to improve conditions for workers in informal and low-wage jobs by providing social protection, ensuring fair wages, and supporting job security.

Why Goal 8 Matters:

Economic growth is essential for reducing poverty, creating jobs, and improving living standards. However, growth must be inclusive and sustainable to benefit everyone and ensure that future generations have equal opportunities. By promoting decent work and economic growth, Goal 8 aims to create a foundation for sustainable development, reduce inequality, and build a more prosperous world for all.

Achieving Goal 8 requires collaboration between governments, businesses, and individuals to foster an environment where people can access decent work, contribute to economic growth, and live dignified lives.

3.2.9 Goal 9: Industry, Innovation, and Infrastructure – Build Resilient Infrastructure, Promote Inclusive and Sustainable Industrialization, and Foster Innovation

Goal 9 of the United Nations Sustainable Development Goals (SDGs) focuses on building resilient infrastructure, promoting sustainable industrialization, and fostering innovation. It aims to create strong, sustainable, and inclusive industries that support economic development, improve technology, and help societies adapt to changes in the global economy.

Key Objectives:

1. **Develop Resilient Infrastructure:** Goal 9 emphasizes the need for developing reliable, sustainable, and modern infrastructure, including transportation networks, energy systems, and information and communication technology (ICT). This is vital for improving access to markets, services, and resources, particularly in developing countries.

2. **Promote Sustainable Industrialization:** The goal encourages industries to adopt sustainable practices that minimize environmental impact, optimize resource use, and promote cleaner production processes. It aims to help industries grow while ensuring they remain environmentally responsible.

3. **Increase Access to Technology and Innovation:** Goal 9 seeks to enhance innovation and the use of new technologies, particularly in emerging industries like green technologies, digital infrastructure, and renewable energy. It promotes the widespread adoption of research and development (R&D) to foster new solutions to global challenges.

4. **Support Small and Medium Enterprises (SMEs):** Goal 9 highlights the importance of supporting small and medium-

sized enterprises (SMEs), as they are crucial for economic growth, job creation, and innovation. This includes providing them with access to finance, technology, and markets.

5. **Promote Research and Development (R&D):** Encouraging investment in R&D helps drive innovation across industries. Goal 9 focuses on enhancing research in fields such as clean energy, sustainable agriculture, and advanced manufacturing.

6. **Upgrade Infrastructure in Developing Countries:** The goal emphasizes the importance of improving infrastructure in low-income and developing countries, helping to bridge the development gap and ensure all nations can participate in the global economy.

7. **Encourage Industrial Diversification and Innovation:** The goal promotes the diversification of industries and encourages innovative approaches that can make industries more efficient, environmentally friendly, and inclusive.

Why Goal 9 Matters:

Industry, innovation, and infrastructure are the backbone of economic development. They provide the foundation for economic growth, create jobs, and improve living standards. By fostering resilient infrastructure and promoting innovation, Goal 9 aims to create sustainable and inclusive industrial development that benefits people and the planet.

Achieving Goal 9 requires collaboration among governments, businesses, and communities to create modern, sustainable industries, advance technological innovation, and build infrastructure that can withstand challenges such as climate change and rapid urbanization.

3.2.10 Goal 10: Reduced Inequalities – Reduce Inequality Within and Among Countries

Goal 10 of the United Nations Sustainable Development Goals (SDGs) focuses on reducing inequalities both within countries and between them. It aims to ensure that everyone, regardless of their background, has the opportunity to improve their well-being and that wealth and resources are distributed more fairly across society.

Key Objectives:

1. **Promote Social, Economic, and Political Inclusion:** Goal 10 seeks to ensure that all people, regardless of race, gender, age, disability, ethnicity, or socioeconomic status, have the opportunity to participate fully in social, economic, and

political life. This includes ensuring equal access to education, healthcare, and employment.

2. **Improve Income Equality:** One of the main focuses of Goal 10 is to reduce income inequality. This involves addressing disparities in wages, wealth, and access to economic opportunities, ensuring that everyone benefits from economic growth and prosperity.

3. **Ensure Equal Opportunities and Access to Resources:** Goal 10 promotes policies and measures that guarantee equal opportunities for all, particularly for marginalized and disadvantaged groups. This includes improving access to social protection, healthcare, education, and affordable housing.

4. **Reduce Discrimination:** The goal aims to combat discrimination based on factors like race, gender, nationality, religion, and disability, ensuring that all individuals are treated fairly and have equal rights and opportunities.

5. **Support Least Developed Countries (LDCs):** Goal 10 encourages richer countries to provide financial and technical support to least developed countries (LDCs) to help reduce inequalities between countries. This includes promoting trade, investment, and debt relief for these nations.

6. **Promote Global Cooperation for Reducing Inequality:** The goal calls for international cooperation to address inequalities on a global scale, through policies that encourage equitable economic growth and foster stronger connections between developed and developing countries.

7. **Improve Migration and Mobility Conditions:** Goal 10 seeks to enhance the conditions for migrants, ensuring they have access to the same rights, protections, and opportunities as local populations, as well as reducing the barriers to mobility.

Why Goal 10 Matters:

Inequality can hinder social and economic progress, perpetuating poverty, limiting access to essential services, and creating barriers to opportunity. Reducing inequalities helps create a more just and fair society, where everyone has the chance to succeed and live fulfilling lives.

Achieving Goal 10 requires global and national efforts to address systemic barriers that create inequality, promote policies that ensure fair distribution of wealth, and ensure equal rights and opportunities for all individuals, leaving no one behind.

3.2.11 Goal 11: Sustainable Cities and Communities – Make Cities and Human Settlements Inclusive, Safe, Resilient, and Sustainable

Goal 11 of the United Nations Sustainable Development Goals (SDGs) focuses on making cities and communities more inclusive, safe, resilient, and sustainable. As more people move to urban areas, it's essential to ensure that cities are well-planned, offer high quality of life, and protect the environment while addressing the needs of all residents.

Key Objectives:

1. **Ensure Access to Affordable Housing:** Goal 11 seeks to make sure that everyone has access to safe, affordable, and adequate housing. This includes addressing the needs of people living in informal settlements and ensuring that housing is built in a way that is safe, resilient, and sustainable.

2. **Promote Sustainable Urbanization:** This goal encourages sustainable city planning and urbanization. It emphasizes using resources efficiently, reducing waste, and minimizing pollution in urban areas while supporting long-term economic, social, and environmental development.

3. **Improve Urban Mobility:** Goal 11 aims to enhance public transportation, making it more accessible and affordable, as well as improving pedestrian and cycling infrastructure. This helps reduce congestion, lowers carbon emissions, and improves quality of life.

4. **Reduce the Environmental Impact of Cities:** The goal calls for reducing the ecological footprint of cities, including improving air quality, managing waste, and conserving natural resources. It also includes strategies for tackling climate change by making cities more resilient to environmental risks such as floods and heatwaves.

5. **Enhance the Safety of Cities:** Goal 11 focuses on reducing crime and violence in urban areas, as well as improving safety in public spaces. It aims to make cities more secure for everyone, particularly women, children, and other vulnerable groups.

6. **Promote Cultural and Natural Heritage Preservation:** This goal encourages preserving cultural heritage, including historic

buildings, landmarks, and natural sites, while ensuring that urban development is done in a way that respects and integrates these resources.

7. **Foster Resilient Infrastructure and Disaster Risk Reduction:** Goal 11 promotes building resilient infrastructure in cities to withstand the impacts of natural disasters, such as floods, earthquakes, and storms. It aims to reduce risks through better preparedness, early warning systems, and emergency response strategies.

8. **Ensure Access to Public Services and Green Spaces:** Goal 11 ensures that all people have access to essential public services, such as water, sanitation, healthcare, and education. It also emphasizes the need for green spaces within cities to improve the well-being of residents and contribute to environmental sustainability.

Why Goal 11 Matters:

Urban areas are home to over half of the world's population and are rapidly growing. Creating cities that are sustainable, resilient, and inclusive is crucial for improving quality of life and ensuring that cities can adapt to future challenges, including climate change, economic growth, and population growth.

Achieving Goal 11 requires collaboration between governments, businesses, and communities to build cities that are livable, equitable, and sustainable for everyone. This includes developing infrastructure, addressing inequality, and protecting the environment for future generations.

3.2.12 Goal 12: Responsible Consumption and Production – Ensure Sustainable Consumption and Production Patterns

Goal 12 of the United Nations Sustainable Development Goals (SDGs) focuses on promoting sustainable consumption and production patterns. It aims to encourage individuals, businesses, and governments to use resources more efficiently and reduce waste while ensuring that economic growth and environmental protection go hand in hand.

Key Objectives:

1. **Reduce Waste Generation:** Goal 12 aims to minimize waste by promoting recycling, reuse, and reducing consumption. This includes managing waste through effective recycling

systems and reducing the amount of plastic, food, and other waste sent to landfills.

2. **Promote Sustainable Resource Use:** This goal encourages the use of natural resources more efficiently and sustainably, including water, energy, and raw materials. It emphasizes the importance of using resources in a way that meets current needs without compromising the ability of future generations to meet theirs.

3. **Encourage Green Technologies and Innovations:** Goal 12 promotes the development and adoption of cleaner, more sustainable technologies. This includes encouraging industries to switch to energy-efficient processes, eco-friendly products, and reducing emissions in their production methods.

4. **Ensure Sustainable Business Practices:** The goal urges businesses to adopt sustainable practices, such as using environmentally-friendly materials, reducing energy consumption, and incorporating social and environmental considerations into their business models.

5. **Promote Sustainable Public Procurement:** Goal 12 encourages governments to implement sustainable public procurement policies. This means purchasing goods and services that are environmentally responsible, socially beneficial, and economically viable.

6. **Increase Public Awareness and Education:** The goal emphasizes the importance of educating people about the environmental impact of their consumption habits and encouraging sustainable choices. This includes promoting eco-friendly lifestyles and raising awareness about the benefits of sustainability.

7. **Support Developing Countries in Achieving Sustainable Consumption:** Goal 12 stresses the importance of supporting developing countries in adopting sustainable consumption and production patterns. This may include providing financial resources, technology, and expertise to help these nations transition to more sustainable practices.

8. **Reduce Environmental Impact of Products:** This objective focuses on reducing the environmental impact of goods and services throughout their life cycle, from production to disposal. It aims to minimize the use of toxic chemicals, reduce emissions, and decrease environmental damage.

Why Goal 12 Matters:
Unsustainable consumption and production practices have led to resource depletion, environmental pollution, and climate change. By promoting responsible consumption and production, Goal 12 seeks to protect the planet's resources while promoting economic growth and improving living standards for all people.

Achieving Goal 12 requires collective action from individuals, industries, governments, and other stakeholders to adopt more sustainable practices. This will ensure that future generations have access to the resources and a healthy environment to thrive in.

3.2.13 Goal 13: Climate Action – Take Urgent Action to Combat Climate Change and Its Impacts

Goal 13 of the United Nations Sustainable Development Goals (SDGs) focuses on taking urgent action to combat climate change and its effects. It aims to address the global challenge of climate change by reducing greenhouse gas emissions, building resilience to its impacts, and promoting climate-conscious policies worldwide.

Key Objectives:

1. **Strengthen Resilience to Climate Impacts:** Goal 13 encourages countries, communities, and businesses to become more resilient to the impacts of climate change. This includes preparing for extreme weather events like floods, droughts, and heatwaves, as well as strengthening infrastructure to cope with these challenges.

2. **Reduce Greenhouse Gas Emissions:** A major goal of Goal 13 is to reduce emissions of greenhouse gases (GHGs), such as carbon dioxide (CO_2), which are the primary drivers of climate change. This involves transitioning to cleaner energy sources, adopting energy-efficient technologies, and promoting low-carbon practices in industries, transportation, and daily life.

3. **Improve Climate Education and Awareness:** Goal 13 emphasizes the importance of educating the public, policymakers, and businesses about climate change and its effects. Increased awareness can lead to more climate-conscious decisions, from individual actions to large-scale policy changes.

4. **Integrate Climate Change Measures into Policies:** Goal 13 calls for the integration of climate change considerations into

national policies, strategies, and plans. This includes aligning development goals with climate action, encouraging sustainable practices, and investing in renewable energy sources.

5. **Promote International Cooperation on Climate Action:** Goal 13 highlights the need for global collaboration in addressing climate change. This includes sharing knowledge, technology, and financial resources, particularly with developing countries, to help them mitigate and adapt to climate change.

6. **Support Climate Change Adaptation and Mitigation Efforts:** Goal 13 encourages investments in adaptation and mitigation measures. Adaptation involves making adjustments to cope with climate change, while mitigation focuses on preventing further damage by reducing emissions and promoting sustainability.

7. **Mobilize Financial Support for Climate Action:** Goal 13 calls for increased financial support to fund climate action projects, particularly in developing countries. This can include investments in renewable energy, climate resilience infrastructure, and sustainable agricultural practices.

8. **Strengthen Early Warning Systems:** Goal 13 emphasizes the importance of improving early warning systems to help communities prepare for climate-related disasters. These systems can reduce risks by providing timely information to those who need it most.

Why Goal 13 Matters:

Climate change is one of the most urgent global challenges of our time, with the potential to cause widespread damage to ecosystems, economies, and societies. Without immediate and substantial action, the effects of climate change—such as rising sea levels, extreme weather, and loss of biodiversity—will worsen, affecting everyone, especially vulnerable populations.

Goal 13 is critical for ensuring a sustainable future for all. By taking action to reduce emissions, enhance resilience, and promote climate-friendly policies, we can limit the damage of climate change and work toward a healthier, more sustainable world for current and future generations.

3.2.14 Goal 14: Life Below Water – Conserve and Sustainably Use the Oceans, Seas, and Marine Resources for Sustainable Development

Goal 14 of the United Nations Sustainable Development Goals (SDGs) focuses on the conservation and sustainable use of the oceans, seas, and marine resources. Oceans cover over 70% of the Earth's surface and are critical to life on Earth, providing food, livelihood, and regulating climate. This goal seeks to protect marine ecosystems and ensure that oceans continue to provide these vital resources for future generations.

Key Objectives:

1. **Prevent and Reduce Marine Pollution:** Goal 14 calls for actions to reduce pollution in oceans and seas, especially from plastics, chemicals, and nutrients that harm marine life. This includes reducing waste entering marine environments and improving waste management systems globally.

2. **Protect Marine and Coastal Ecosystems:** The goal aims to safeguard marine and coastal ecosystems, including coral reefs, mangroves, and coastal wetlands. These ecosystems provide essential services such as carbon sequestration, biodiversity, and coastal protection from storms.

3. **Minimize Ocean Acidification:** Goal 14 encourages efforts to address ocean acidification, which occurs when excess carbon dioxide is absorbed by oceans, harming marine life, especially shellfish and coral reefs. Reducing emissions of CO2 can help slow down this process.

4. **Sustainable Fisheries Management:** Goal 14 promotes the sustainable management of fisheries to prevent overfishing, protect marine species, and ensure the long-term health of ocean ecosystems. This includes enforcing fishing regulations, promoting sustainable aquaculture, and ending harmful fishing practices.

5. **Increase Marine Protected Areas:** Expanding the number and size of marine protected areas (MPAs) helps preserve biodiversity and safeguard critical habitats from human activity. MPAs are areas where fishing and other harmful activities are restricted or banned to protect marine life.

6. **Promote Sustainable Ocean-based Economies:** Goal 14 encourages the development of sustainable industries that rely on ocean resources, such as tourism, fishing, and renewable

energy. This includes promoting practices that do not harm marine ecosystems and ensure that communities can benefit from ocean resources in the long term.

7. **Enhance Scientific Research and Knowledge:** Goal 14 highlights the importance of scientific research to better understand oceans, seas, and marine resources. This includes improving data collection, monitoring marine biodiversity, and sharing knowledge about marine ecosystems and their sustainability.

8. **Increase International Cooperation for Ocean Conservation:** Goal 14 stresses the need for global cooperation to tackle marine issues. This includes sharing resources, knowledge, and technology to protect oceans and address global marine challenges.

Why Goal 14 Matters:

Oceans are a vital part of Earth's systems, providing food, regulating the climate, and supporting biodiversity. However, they face numerous threats, including pollution, overfishing, and habitat destruction, which jeopardize marine life and the benefits humans derive from the oceans. Goal 14 is crucial for ensuring the health of oceans, seas, and marine life for future generations. By adopting sustainable practices, protecting marine ecosystems, and reducing pollution, we can ensure that oceans continue to support life on Earth and contribute to the global economy. Achieving this goal requires collective global action, scientific innovation, and effective governance to protect marine resources.

3.2.15 Goal 15: Life on Land – Protect, Restore, and Promote Sustainable Use of Terrestrial Ecosystems, Sustainably Manage Forests, Combat Desertification, Halt and Reverse Land Degradation, and Halt Biodiversity Loss

Goal 15 of the United Nations Sustainable Development Goals (SDGs) focuses on the conservation, restoration, and sustainable use of terrestrial ecosystems, including forests, wetlands, drylands, and mountains. This goal aims to ensure that land resources are managed in a way that maintains biodiversity, prevents degradation, and contributes to sustainable development.

Key Objectives:

1. **Protect and Restore Ecosystems and Biodiversity:** Goal 15 emphasizes the importance of protecting and restoring

terrestrial ecosystems, such as forests, grasslands, and wetlands, which are crucial for biodiversity. This includes protecting endangered species and promoting the restoration of degraded habitats.

2. **Sustainable Forest Management:** The goal promotes the sustainable management of forests, which are vital for carbon sequestration, biodiversity, and livelihoods. It encourages reforestation, afforestation, and reducing deforestation, while ensuring that forests are used in a way that maintains their ecological functions.

3. **Combat Desertification and Land Degradation:** Goal 15 focuses on combating desertification and land degradation, particularly in drylands and arid regions. This includes implementing sustainable land management practices that prevent soil erosion, improve soil fertility, and protect land from overuse and desertification.

4. **Promote Sustainable Agriculture:** Goal 15 encourages the adoption of sustainable agricultural practices that preserve land quality, enhance food security, and reduce the environmental impact of farming. This includes techniques like crop rotation, agroforestry, and organic farming that promote soil health and biodiversity.

5. **Prevent Poaching and Halt Biodiversity Loss:** Goal 15 works toward halting the loss of biodiversity caused by illegal hunting, poaching, and habitat destruction. It also emphasizes strengthening laws to protect wildlife and promoting conservation efforts for endangered species.

6. **Ensure Access to Genetic Resources and Traditional Knowledge:** The goal highlights the importance of ensuring fair and equitable access to genetic resources and traditional knowledge, especially for indigenous communities. This includes respecting intellectual property rights related to biodiversity and ensuring that communities benefit from the use of their resources.

7. **Promote the Sustainable Use of Land and Resources:** Goal 15 encourages sustainable land use practices that balance economic development with the protection of natural resources. This includes sustainable land planning, urban development, and the responsible extraction of resources.

8. **Increase International Cooperation for Land Conservation:** Goal 15 emphasizes the need for global collaboration to conserve and restore terrestrial ecosystems. It encourages countries to work together on issues like biodiversity loss, desertification, and land management.

Why Goal 15 Matters:

Healthy land ecosystems are essential for the survival of all life on Earth. They provide food, water, and resources, support biodiversity, and help regulate the climate. However, deforestation, desertification, and land degradation threaten these vital ecosystems, which can have devastating effects on human health, livelihoods, and food security.

Goal 15 is critical for protecting the Earth's biodiversity and natural resources for future generations. By adopting sustainable land management practices, restoring degraded ecosystems, and protecting wildlife, we can ensure that ecosystems continue to provide essential services and contribute to sustainable development. Achieving this goal requires coordinated efforts at the local, national, and international levels to address the many challenges facing terrestrial ecosystems.

3.2.16 Goal 16: Peace, Justice, and Strong Institutions – Promote Peaceful and Inclusive Societies for Sustainable Development, Provide Access to Justice for All, and Build Effective, Accountable, and Inclusive Institutions at All Levels

Goal 16 of the United Nations Sustainable Development Goals (SDGs) focuses on promoting peace, justice, and strong institutions. It aims to ensure that all individuals live in peaceful societies where their rights are protected, justice is accessible, and institutions are transparent, accountable, and inclusive.

Key Objectives:

1. **Promote the Rule of Law and Access to Justice:** Goal 16 emphasizes the importance of ensuring that laws are fair, accessible, and applied equally to all people. It aims to strengthen legal systems, provide access to justice for everyone, and protect individuals' rights, especially those from marginalized groups.

2. **Reduce Violence and Foster Peace:** Goal 16 seeks to reduce all forms of violence, including armed conflict, domestic violence, and organized crime. It aims to foster peaceful

societies where individuals and communities live free from fear, violence, and conflict.

3. **Strengthen Institutions at All Levels:** The goal calls for strengthening national and local institutions, including governments, the judiciary, and law enforcement, to ensure that they are effective, accountable, and responsive to the needs of society. This includes promoting transparency and reducing corruption.

4. **Promote Inclusive Decision-Making:** Goal 16 advocates for inclusive, participatory decision-making processes where all people, including women, youth, and marginalized groups, have a voice in political and public matters. This includes enhancing political participation, representation, and ensuring that decisions are made for the benefit of all.

5. **Combat Corruption and Bribery:** The goal aims to reduce corruption and bribery in both the public and private sectors. Strengthening laws and practices that promote transparency, accountability, and integrity can help ensure that resources are used for the public good.

6. **Ensure the Protection of Fundamental Freedoms:** Goal 16 seeks to protect and promote the fundamental freedoms and rights of all individuals, including freedom of speech, assembly, and association. It calls for safeguarding individuals' ability to speak out, participate in society, and access information.

7. **Strengthen International Cooperation for Peace and Justice:** The goal encourages international collaboration to promote peace and justice, addressing global issues such as cross-border crime, conflict resolution, and human rights protection. This includes enhancing the role of the United Nations and other international organizations in maintaining peace and stability.

8. **Promote the Establishment of Effective Institutions:** Goal 16 promotes the creation of institutions that are capable of delivering services efficiently and equitably. These institutions should be able to manage resources responsibly, implement policies effectively, and respond to public needs in a fair and just manner.

Why Goal 16 Matters:

Peaceful societies with strong institutions are the foundation for sustainable development. Without peace, justice, and effective governance, it is difficult to achieve economic growth, protect human rights, and create a stable environment for individuals and communities to thrive. Weak institutions, corruption, and violence undermine development and hinder progress in other areas, such as health, education, and environmental protection.

Goal 16 is vital because it creates the environment necessary for sustainable development to take place. It ensures that people have the opportunity to live in societies where their rights are protected, justice is accessible, and institutions work for the benefit of everyone. Achieving this goal requires a collective effort from governments, civil society, and individuals to create just, inclusive, and peaceful societies.

3.2.17 Goal 17: Partnerships for the Goals – Strengthen the Means of Implementation and Revitalize the Global Partnership for Sustainable Development

Goal 17 of the United Nations Sustainable Development Goals (SDGs) focuses on strengthening global partnerships and cooperation to achieve all the SDGs. It recognizes that achieving sustainable development requires collective action and a commitment from governments, businesses, civil society, and individuals worldwide. This goal seeks to ensure that all countries, particularly developing ones, have the support they need to achieve sustainable development.

Key Objectives:

1. **Finance for Sustainable Development:** Goal 17 calls for increased financial support for sustainable development initiatives. This includes mobilizing financial resources from both public and private sources, ensuring that funds are available for projects that advance the SDGs, especially in developing countries.

2. **Technology and Innovation:** The goal emphasizes the importance of technology, innovation, and knowledge-sharing in achieving the SDGs. It aims to ensure that developing countries have access to affordable technologies, expertise, and innovation to solve key challenges such as poverty, health, and environmental sustainability.

3. **Capacity-Building:** Goal 17 focuses on building the capacities of developing countries, particularly those with limited resources, to effectively implement the SDGs. This

includes strengthening human resources, institutional frameworks, and skills training, as well as fostering partnerships for knowledge exchange and collaboration.

4. **Trade and Policy Coherence:** The goal encourages international trade policies that are fair and supportive of sustainable development. It aims to improve global trade practices and ensure that they contribute to sustainable economic growth, poverty reduction, and the overall achievement of the SDGs.

5. **Promote Global Partnerships:** Goal 17 calls for the strengthening of multi-stakeholder partnerships that involve governments, businesses, academia, and civil society. These partnerships should work together to create innovative solutions and implement projects that contribute to the SDGs, especially in areas like healthcare, education, and climate change.

6. **Data, Monitoring, and Accountability:** The goal promotes the collection and use of data to track progress toward achieving the SDGs. By strengthening national statistical systems and improving data sharing, countries can better monitor their development progress and ensure transparency and accountability in implementation.

7. **Private Sector Engagement:** Goal 17 encourages the private sector to play an active role in achieving the SDGs. This includes encouraging businesses to adopt sustainable practices, invest in green technologies, and engage in partnerships that contribute to social, environmental, and economic development.

8. **Inclusive Global Governance:** The goal calls for strengthening global governance systems, including the United Nations and other international organizations, to ensure that they effectively address global challenges and support the achievement of the SDGs. It encourages inclusive decision-making processes where all stakeholders are involved.

Why Goal 17 Matters:

No country can achieve the SDGs alone. Global challenges such as climate change, inequality, and health crises require coordinated efforts across borders. Goal 17 highlights the importance of partnerships between governments, businesses, and civil society to create a shared responsibility for sustainable development. By strengthening partnerships and improving cooperation, we can achieve greater impact and ensure that no one is left behind in the pursuit of the SDGs. This goal is essential because it recognizes that the success of the SDGs depends on collective action and collaboration. By building stronger partnerships, improving access to resources, sharing knowledge and technology, and fostering accountability, Goal 17 aims to create the conditions necessary for the successful implementation of all other SDGs.

3.3 Overview of Indicators Used to Measure Progress

Sustainable Development Goal indicators should be disaggregated, where relevant, by income, sex, age, race, ethnicity, migratory status, disability and geographic location, or other characteristics, in accordance with the Fundamental Principles of Official Statistics. Table 4.1 details the indicators used to track progress toward the United Nations Sustainable Development Goals (SDGs). These indicators are organized according to their respective SDGs.

Table 3.2: Global indicator framework for the Sustainable Development Goals and targets of the 2030 Agenda for Sustainable Development.

Goals and targets (from the 2030 Agenda)	*Indicators*
Goal 1. End poverty in all its forms everywhere	
1.1 By 2030, eradicate extreme poverty for all people everywhere, currently measured as people living on less than $1.25 a day	1.1.1 Proportion of population below the international poverty line, by sex, age, employment status and geographical location (urban/rural)
1.2 By 2030, reduce at least by half the proportion of men, women and children of all ages living in poverty in all its dimensions according to national definitions	1.2.1 Proportion of population living below the national poverty line, by sex and age
	1.2.2 Proportion of men, women and children of all ages living in poverty in all its dimensions according to national definitions
1.3 Implement nationally appropriate social protection systems and measures for all, including floors, and by 2030 achieve substantial coverage of the poor and the vulnerable	1.3.1 Proportion of population covered by social protection floors/systems, by sex, distinguishing children, unemployed persons, older persons, persons with disabilities, pregnant women, newborns, work-injury victims and the poor and the vulnerable
1.4 By 2030, ensure that all men and women, in particular the poor and the vulnerable, have equal rights to	1.4.1 Proportion of population living in households with access to basic services

economic resources, as well as access to basic services, ownership and control over land and other forms of property, inheritance, natural resources, appropriate new technology and financial services, including microfinance	1.4.2 Proportion of total adult population with secure tenure rights to land, with legally recognized documentation and who perceive their rights to land as secure, by sex and by type of tenure
1.5 By 2030, build the resilience of the poor and those in vulnerable situations and reduce their exposure and vulnerability to climate-related extreme events and other economic, social and environmental shocks and disasters	1.5.1 Number of deaths, missing persons and persons affected by disaster per 100,000 people[a]
	1.5.2 Direct disaster economic loss in relation to global gross domestic product (GDP)[a]
	1.5.3 Number of countries with national and local disaster risk reduction strategies[a]
1.a Ensure significant mobilization of resources from a variety of sources, including through enhanced development cooperation, in order to provide adequate and predictable means for developing countries, in particular least developed countries, to implement programmes and policies to end poverty in all its dimensions	1.a.1 Proportion of resources allocated by the government directly to poverty reduction programmes
	1.a.2 Proportion of total government spending on essential services (education, health and social protection)
1.b Create sound policy frameworks at the national, regional and international levels, based on pro-poor and gender-sensitive development strategies, to support accelerated investment in poverty eradication actions	1.b.1 Proportion of government recurrent and capital spending to sectors that disproportionately benefit women, the poor and vulnerable groups
Goal 2. End hunger, achieve food security and improved nutrition and promote sustainable agriculture	
2.1 By 2030, end hunger and ensure access by all people, in particular the poor and people in vulnerable situations, including infants, to safe, nutritious and sufficient food all year round	2.1.1 Prevalence of undernourishment
	2.1.2 Prevalence of moderate or severe food insecurity in the population, based on the Food Insecurity Experience Scale (FIES)
2.2 By 2030, end all forms of malnutrition, including achieving, by 2025, the internationally agreed targets on stunting and wasting in children under 5 years of age, and address the nutritional needs of adolescent girls, pregnant and lactating women and older persons	2.2.1 Prevalence of stunting (height for age <-2 standard deviation from the median of the World Health Organization (WHO) Child Growth Standards) among children under 5 years of age
	2.2.2 Prevalence of malnutrition (weight for height >+2 or <-2 standard deviation from the median of the WHO Child Growth Standards) among children under 5

	years of age, by type (wasting and overweight)
2.3 By 2030, double the agricultural productivity and incomes of small-scale food producers, in particular women, indigenous peoples, family farmers, pastoralists and fishers, including through secure and equal access to land, other productive resources and inputs, knowledge, financial services, markets and opportunities for value addition and non-farm employment	2.3.1 Volume of production per labour unit by classes of farming/pastoral/forestry enterprise size
	2.3.2 Average income of small-scale food producers, by sex and indigenous status
2.4 By 2030, ensure sustainable food production systems and implement resilient agricultural practices that increase productivity and production, that help maintain ecosystems, that strengthen capacity for adaptation to climate change, extreme weather, drought, flooding and other disasters and that progressively improve land and soil quality	2.4.1 Proportion of agricultural area under productive and sustainable agriculture
2.5 By 2020, maintain the genetic diversity of seeds, cultivated plants and farmed and domesticated animals and their related wild species, including through soundly managed and diversified seed and plant banks at the national, regional and international levels, and promote access to and fair and equitable sharing of benefits arising from the utilization of genetic resources and associated traditional knowledge, as internationally agreed	2.5.1 Number of plant and animal genetic resources for food and agriculture secured in either medium or long-term conservation facilities
	2.5.2 Proportion of local breeds classified as being at risk, not-at-risk or at unknown level of risk of extinction
2.a Increase investment, including through enhanced international cooperation, in rural infrastructure, agricultural research and extension services, technology development and plant and livestock gene banks in order to enhance agricultural productive capacity in developing countries, in particular least developed countries	2.a.1 The agriculture orientation index for government expenditures
	2.a.2 Total official flows (official development assistance plus other official flows) to the agriculture sector
2.b Correct and prevent trade restrictions and distortions in world agricultural markets, including through the parallel elimination of all forms of agricultural export subsidies and all export measures with equivalent effect,	2.b.1 Producer Support Estimate
	2.b.2 Agricultural export subsidies

in accordance with the mandate of the Doha Development Round	
2.c Adopt measures to ensure the proper functioning of food commodity markets and their derivatives and facilitate timely access to market information, including on food reserves, in order to help limit extreme food price volatility	2.c.1 Indicator of food price anomalies
Goal 3. Ensure healthy lives and promote well-being for all at all ages	
3.1 By 2030, reduce the global maternal mortality ratio to less than 70 per 100,000 live births	3.1.1 Maternal mortality ratio
	3.1.2 Proportion of births attended by skilled health personnel
3.2 By 2030, end preventable deaths of newborns and children under 5 years of age, with all countries aiming to reduce neonatal mortality to at least as low as 12 per 1,000 live births and under-5 mortality to at least as low as 25 per 1,000 live births	3.2.1 Under-five mortality rate
	3.2.2 Neonatal mortality rate
3.3 By 2030, end the epidemics of AIDS, tuberculosis, malaria and neglected tropical diseases and combat hepatitis, water-borne diseases and other communicable diseases	3.3.1 Number of new HIV infections per 1,000 uninfected population, by sex, age and key populations
	3.3.2 Tuberculosis incidence per 1,000 population
	3.3.3 Malaria incidence per 1,000 population
	3.3.4 Hepatitis B incidence per 100,000 population
	3.3.5 Number of people requiring interventions against neglected tropical diseases
3.4 By 2030, reduce by one third premature mortality from non-communicable diseases through prevention and treatment and promote mental health and well-being	3.4.1 Mortality rate attributed to cardiovascular disease, cancer, diabetes or chronic respiratory disease
	3.4.2 Suicide mortality rate
3.5 Strengthen the prevention and treatment of substance abuse, including narcotic drug abuse and harmful use of alcohol	3.5.1 Coverage of treatment interventions (pharmacological, psychosocial and rehabilitation and aftercare services) for substance use disorders
	3.5.2 Harmful use of alcohol, defined according to the national context as alcohol per capita consumption (aged 15 years and older) within a calendar year in litres of pure alcohol
3.6 By 2020, halve the number of	3.6.1 Death rate due to road traffic

global deaths and injuries from road traffic accidents	injuries
3.7 By 2030, ensure universal access to sexual and reproductive health-care services, including for family planning, information and education, and the integration of reproductive health into national strategies and programmes	3.7.1 Proportion of women of reproductive age (aged 15-49 years) who have their need for family planning satisfied with modern methods
	3.7.2 Adolescent birth rate (aged 10-14 years; aged 15-19 years) per 1,000 women in that age group
3.8 Achieve universal health coverage, including financial risk protection, access to quality essential health-care services and access to safe, effective, quality and affordable essential medicines and vaccines for all	3.8.1 Coverage of essential health services (defined as the average coverage of essential services based on tracer interventions that include reproductive, maternal, newborn and child health, infectious diseases, non-communicable diseases and service capacity and access, among the general and the most disadvantaged population)
	3.8.2 Number of people covered by health insurance or a public health system per 1,000 population
3.9 By 2030, substantially reduce the number of deaths and illnesses from hazardous chemicals and air, water and soil pollution and contamination	3.9.1 Mortality rate attributed to household and ambient air pollution
	3.9.2 Mortality rate attributed to unsafe water, unsafe sanitation and lack of hygiene (exposure to unsafe Water, Sanitation and Hygiene for All (WASH) services)
	3.9.3 Mortality rate attributed to unintentional poisoning
3.a Strengthen the implementation of the World Health Organization Framework Convention on Tobacco Control in all countries, as appropriate	3.a.1 Age-standardized prevalence of current tobacco use among persons aged 15 years and older
3.b Support the research and development of vaccines and medicines for the communicable and non-communicable diseases that primarily affect developing countries, provide access to affordable essential medicines and vaccines, in accordance with the Doha Declaration on the TRIPS Agreement and Public Health, which affirms the right of developing countries to use to the full the provisions in the Agreement on Trade-Related Aspects of Intellectual Property Rights regarding flexibilities	3.b.1 Proportion of the population with access to affordable medicines and vaccines on a sustainable basis
	3.b.2 Total net official development assistance to medical research and basic health sectors

to protect public health, and, in particular, provide access to medicines for all	
3.c Substantially increase health financing and the recruitment, development, training and retention of the health workforce in developing countries, especially in least developed countries and small island developing States	3.c.1 Health worker density and distribution
3.d Strengthen the capacity of all countries, in particular developing countries, for early warning, risk reduction and management of national and global health risks	3.d.1 International Health Regulations (IHR) capacity and health emergency preparedness
Goal 4. Ensure inclusive and equitable quality education and promote lifelong learning opportunities for all	
4.1 By 2030, ensure that all girls and boys complete free, equitable and quality primary and secondary education leading to relevant and effective learning outcomes	4.1.1 Proportion of children and young people: (a) in grades 2/3; (b) at the end of primary; and (c) at the end of lower secondary achieving at least a minimum proficiency level in (i) reading and (ii) mathematics, by sex
4.2 By 2030, ensure that all girls and boys have access to quality early childhood development, care and pre-primary education so that they are ready for primary education	4.2.1 Proportion of children under 5 years of age who are developmentally on track in health, learning and psychosocial well-being, by sex
	4.2.2 Participation rate in organized learning (one year before the official primary entry age), by sex
4.3 By 2030, ensure equal access for all women and men to affordable and quality technical, vocational and tertiary education, including university	4.3.1 Participation rate of youth and adults in formal and non-formal education and training in the previous 12 months, by sex
4.4 By 2030, substantially increase the number of youth and adults who have relevant skills, including technical and vocational skills, for employment, decent jobs and entrepreneurship	4.4.1 Proportion of youth and adults with information and communications technology (ICT) skills, by type of skill
4.5 By 2030, eliminate gender disparities in education and ensure equal access to all levels of education and vocational training for the vulnerable, including persons with disabilities, indigenous peoples and children in vulnerable situations	4.5.1 Parity indices (female/male, rural/urban, bottom/top wealth quintile and others such as disability status, indigenous peoples and conflict-affected, as data become available) for all education indicators on this list that can be disaggregated
4.6 By 2030, ensure that all youth and	4.6.1 Percentage of population in a

a substantial proportion of adults, both men and women, achieve literacy and numeracy	given age group achieving at least a fixed level of proficiency in functional (a) literacy and (b) numeracy skills, by sex
4.7 By 2030, ensure that all learners acquire the knowledge and skills needed to promote sustainable development, including, among others, through education for sustainable development and sustainable lifestyles, human rights, gender equality, promotion of a culture of peace and non-violence, global citizenship and appreciation of cultural diversity and of culture's contribution to sustainable development	4.7.1 Extent to which (i) global citizenship education and (ii) education for sustainable development, including gender equality and human rights, are mainstreamed at all levels in: (a) national education policies, (b) curricula, (c) teacher education and (d) student assessment
4.a Build and upgrade education facilities that are child, disability and gender sensitive and provide safe, non-violent, inclusive and effective learning environments for all	4.a.1 Proportion of schools with access to: (a) electricity; (b) the Internet for pedagogical purposes; (c) computers for pedagogical purposes; (d) adapted infrastructure and materials for students with disabilities; (e) basic drinking water; (f) single-sex basic sanitation facilities; and (g) basic handwashing facilities (as per the WASH indicator definitions)
4.b By 2020, substantially expand globally the number of scholarships available to developing countries, in particular least developed countries, small island developing States and African countries, for enrolment in higher education, including vocational training and information and communications technology, technical, engineering and scientific programmes, in developed countries and other developing countries	4.b.1 Volume of official development assistance flows for scholarships by sector and type of study
4.c By 2030, substantially increase the supply of qualified teachers, including through international cooperation for teacher training in developing countries, especially least developed countries and small island developing States	4.c.1 Proportion of teachers in: (a) pre-primary; (b) primary; (c) lower secondary; and (d) upper secondary education who have received at least the minimum organized teacher training (e.g. pedagogical training) pre-service or in-service required for teaching at the relevant level in a given country
Goal 5. Achieve gender equality and empower all women and girls	
5.1 End all forms of discrimination	5.1.1 Whether or not legal

against all women and girls everywhere	frameworks are in place to promote, enforce and monitor equality and non-discrimination on the basis of sex
5.2 Eliminate all forms of violence against all women and girls in the public and private spheres, including trafficking and sexual and other types of exploitation	5.2.1 Proportion of ever-partnered women and girls aged 15 years and older subjected to physical, sexual or psychological violence by a current or former intimate partner in the previous 12 months, by form of violence and by age
	5.2.2 Proportion of women and girls aged 15 years and older subjected to sexual violence by persons other than an intimate partner in the previous 12 months, by age and place of occurrence
5.3 Eliminate all harmful practices, such as child, early and forced marriage and female genital mutilation	5.3.1 Proportion of women aged 20-24 years who were married or in a union before age 15 and before age 18
	5.3.2 Proportion of girls and women aged 15-49 years who have undergone female genital mutilation/cutting, by age
5.4 Recognize and value unpaid care and domestic work through the provision of public services, infrastructure and social protection policies and the promotion of shared responsibility within the household and the family as nationally appropriate	5.4.1 Proportion of time spent on unpaid domestic and care work, by sex, age and location
5.5 Ensure women's full and effective participation and equal opportunities for leadership at all levels of decision-making in political, economic and public life	5.5.1 Proportion of seats held by women in national parliaments and local governments
	5.5.2 Proportion of women in managerial positions
5.6 Ensure universal access to sexual and reproductive health and reproductive rights as agreed in accordance with the Programme of Action of the International Conference on Population and Development and the Beijing Platform for Action and the outcome documents of their review conferences	5.6.1 Proportion of women aged 15-49 years who make their own informed decisions regarding sexual relations, contraceptive use and reproductive health care
	5.6.2 Number of countries with laws and regulations that guarantee women aged 15-49 years access to sexual and reproductive health care, information and education
5.a Undertake reforms to give women equal rights to economic resources, as	5.a.1 (a) Proportion of total agricultural population with

well as access to ownership and control over land and other forms of property, financial services, inheritance and natural resources, in accordance with national laws	ownership or secure rights over agricultural land, by sex; and (b) share of women among owners or rights-bearers of agricultural land, by type of tenure
	5.a.2 Proportion of countries where the legal framework (including customary law) guarantees women's equal rights to land ownership and/or control
5.b Enhance the use of enabling technology, in particular information and communications technology, to promote the empowerment of women	5.b.1 Proportion of individuals who own a mobile telephone, by sex
5.c Adopt and strengthen sound policies and enforceable legislation for the promotion of gender equality and the empowerment of all women and girls at all levels	5.c.1 Proportion of countries with systems to track and make public allocations for gender equality and women's empowerment
Goal 6. Ensure availability and sustainable management of water and sanitation for all	
6.1 By 2030, achieve universal and equitable access to safe and affordable drinking water for all	6.1.1 Proportion of population using safely managed drinking water services
6.2 By 2030, achieve access to adequate and equitable sanitation and hygiene for all and end open defecation, paying special attention to the needs of women and girls and those in vulnerable situations	6.2.1 Proportion of population using safely managed sanitation services, including a hand-washing facility with soap and water
6.3 By 2030, improve water quality by reducing pollution, eliminating dumping and minimizing release of hazardous chemicals and materials, halving the proportion of untreated wastewater and substantially increasing recycling and safe reuse globally	6.3.1 Proportion of wastewater safely treated
	6.3.2 Proportion of bodies of water with good ambient water quality
6.4 By 2030, substantially increase water-use efficiency across all sectors and ensure sustainable withdrawals and supply of freshwater to address water scarcity and substantially reduce the number of people suffering from water scarcity	6.4.1 Change in water-use efficiency over time
	6.4.2 Level of water stress: freshwater withdrawal as a proportion of available freshwater resources
6.5 By 2030, implement integrated water resources management at all levels, including through transboundary cooperation as appropriate	6.5.1Degree of integrated water resources management implementation (0-100)
	6.5.2 Proportion of transboundary basin area with an operational

	arrangement for water cooperation
6.6 By 2020, protect and restore water-related ecosystems, including mountains, forests, wetlands, rivers, aquifers and lakes	6.6.1 Change in the extent of water-related ecosystems over time
6.a By 2030, expand international cooperation and capacity-building support to developing countries in water- and sanitation-related activities and programmes, including water harvesting, desalination, water efficiency, wastewater treatment, recycling and reuse technologies	6.a.1 Amount of water- and sanitation-related official development assistance that is part of a government-coordinated spending plan
6.b Support and strengthen the participation of local communities in improving water and sanitation management	6.b.1 Proportion of local administrative units with established and operational policies and procedures for participation of local communities in water and sanitation management

Goal 7. Ensure access to affordable, reliable, sustainable and modern energy for all

7.1 By 2030, ensure universal access to affordable, reliable and modern energy services	7.1.1 Proportion of population with access to electricity
	7.1.2 Proportion of population with primary reliance on clean fuels and technology
7.2 By 2030, increase substantially the share of renewable energy in the global energy mix	7.2.1 Renewable energy share in the total final energy consumption
7.3 By 2030, double the global rate of improvement in energy efficiency	7.3.1 Energy intensity measured in terms of primary energy and GDP
7.a By 2030, enhance international cooperation to facilitate access to clean energy research and technology, including renewable energy, energy efficiency and advanced and cleaner fossil-fuel technology, and promote investment in energy infrastructure and clean energy technology	7.a.1 Mobilizedamount of United States dollars per year starting in 2020 accountable towards the $100 billion commitment
7.b By 2030, expand infrastructure and upgrade technology for supplying modern and sustainable energy services for all in developing countries, in particular least developed countries, small island developing States and landlocked developing countries, in accordance with their respective programmes of support	7.b.1 Investments in energy efficiency as a percentage of GDP and the amount of foreign direct investment in financial transfer for infrastructure and technology to sustainable development services

Goal 8. Promote sustained, inclusive and sustainable economic growth, full and productive employment and decent work for all

8.1 Sustain per capita economic growth in accordance with national circumstances and, in particular, at least 7 per cent gross domestic product growth per annum in the least developed countries	8.1.1 Annual growth rate of real GDP per capita
8.2 Achieve higher levels of economic productivity through diversification, technological upgrading and innovation, including through a focus on high-value added and labour-intensive sectors	8.2.1 Annual growth rate of real GDP per employed person
8.3 Promote development-oriented policies that support productive activities, decent job creation, entrepreneurship, creativity and innovation, and encourage the formalization and growth of micro-, small- and medium-sized enterprises, including through access to financial services	8.3.1 Proportion of informal employment in non-agriculture employment, by sex
8.4 Improve progressively, through 2030, global resource efficiency in consumption and production and endeavour to decouple economic growth from environmental degradation, in accordance with the 10-Year Framework of Programmes on Sustainable Consumption and Production, with developed countries taking the lead	8.4.1 Material footprint, material footprint per capita, and material footprint per GDP
	8.4.2 Domestic material consumption, domestic material consumption per capita, and domestic material consumption per GDP
8.5 By 2030, achieve full and productive employment and decent work for all women and men, including for young people and persons with disabilities, and equal pay for work of equal value	8.5.1 Average hourly earnings of female and male employees, by occupation, age and persons with disabilities
	8.5.2 Unemployment rate, by sex, age and persons with disabilities
8.6 By 2020, substantially reduce the proportion of youth not in employment, education or training	8.6.1 Proportion of youth (aged 15-24 years) not in education, employment or training
8.7 Take immediate and effective measures to eradicate forced labour, end modern slavery and human trafficking and secure the prohibition and elimination of the worst forms of child labour, including recruitment and use of child soldiers, and by 2025 end child labour in all its forms	8.7.1 Proportion and number of children aged 5-17 years engaged in child labour, by sex and age
8.8 Protect labour rights and promote safe and secure working environments	8.8.1 Frequency rates of fatal and non-fatal occupational injuries, by

for all workers, including migrant workers, in particular women migrants, and those in precarious employment	sex and migrant status
	8.8.2 Increase in national compliance of labour rights (freedom of association and collective bargaining) based on International Labour Organization (ILO) textual sources and national legislation, by sex and migrant status
8.9 By 2030, devise and implement policies to promote sustainable tourism that creates jobs and promotes local culture and products	8.9.1 Tourism direct GDP as a proportion of total GDP and in growth rate
	8.9.2 Number of jobs in tourism industries as a proportion of total jobs and growth rate of jobs, by sex
8.10 Strengthen the capacity of domestic financial institutions to encourage and expand access to banking, insurance and financial services for all	8.10.1 Number of commercial bank branches and automated teller machines (ATMs) per 100,000 adults
	8.10.2 Proportion of adults (15 years and older) with an account at a bank or other financial institution or with a mobile-money-service provider
8.a Increase Aid for Trade support for developing countries, in particular least developed countries, including through the Enhanced Integrated Framework for Trade-related Technical Assistance to Least Developed Countries	8.a.1 Aid for Trade commitments and disbursements
8.b By 2020, develop and operationalize a global strategy for youth employment and implement the Global Jobs Pact of the International Labour Organization	8.b.1 Total government spending in social protection and employment programmes as a proportion of the national budgets and GDP
Goal 9. Build resilient infrastructure, promote inclusive and sustainable industrialization and foster innovation	
9.1 Develop quality, reliable, sustainable and resilient infrastructure, including regional and trans-border infrastructure, to support economic development and human well-being, with a focus on affordable and equitable access for all	9.1.1 Proportion of the rural population who live within 2 km of an all-season road
	9.1.2 Passenger and freight volumes, by mode of transport
9.2 Promote inclusive and sustainable industrialization and, by 2030, significantly raise industry's share of employment and gross domestic product, in line with national	9.2.1 Manufacturing value added as a proportion of GDP and per capita
	9.2.2 Manufacturing employment as a proportion of total employment

circumstances, and double its share in least developed countries	
9.3 Increase the access of small-scale industrial and other enterprises, in particular in developing countries, to financial services, including affordable credit, and their integration into value chains and markets	9.3.1 Proportion of small-scale industries in total industry value added
	9.3.2 Proportion of small-scale industries with a loan or line of credit
9.4 By 2030, upgrade infrastructure and retrofit industries to make them sustainable, with increased resource-use efficiency and greater adoption of clean and environmentally sound technologies and industrial processes, with all countries taking action in accordance with their respective capabilities	9.4.1 CO_2 emission per unit of value added
9.5 Enhance scientific research, upgrade the technological capabilities of industrial sectors in all countries, in particular developing countries, including, by 2030, encouraging innovation and substantially increasing the number of research and development workers per 1 million people and public and private research and development spending	9.5.1 Research and development expenditure as a proportion of GDP
	9.5.2 Researchers (in full-time equivalent) per million inhabitants
9.a Facilitate sustainable and resilient infrastructure development in developing countries through enhanced financial, technological and technical support to African countries, least developed countries, landlocked developing countries and small island developing States	9.a.1 Total official international support (official development assistance plus other official flows) to infrastructure
9.b Support domestic technology development, research and innovation in developing countries, including by ensuring a conducive policy environment for, inter alia, industrial diversification and value addition to commodities	9.b.1 Proportion of medium and high-tech industry value added in total value added
9.c Significantly increase access to information and communications technology and strive to provide universal and affordable access to the Internet in least developed countries by 2020	9.c.1 Proportion of population covered by a mobile network, by technology
Goal 10. Reduce inequality within and among countries	
10.1 By 2030, progressively achieve	10.1.1 Growth rates of household

and sustain income growth of the bottom 40 per cent of the population at a rate higher than the national average	expenditure or income per capita among the bottom 40 per cent of the population and the total population
10.2 By 2030, empower and promote the social, economic and political inclusion of all, irrespective of age, sex, disability, race, ethnicity, origin, religion or economic or other status	10.2.1 Proportion of people living below 50 per cent of median income, by age, sex and persons with disabilities
10.3 Ensure equal opportunity and reduce inequalities of outcome, including by eliminating discriminatory laws, policies and practices and promoting appropriate legislation, policies and action in this regard	10.3.1 Proportion of the population reporting having personally felt discriminated against or harassed within the previous 12 months on the basis of a ground of discrimination prohibited under international human rights law
10.4 Adopt policies, especially fiscal, wage and social protection policies, and progressively achieve greater equality	10.4.1 Labour share of GDP, comprising wages and social protection transfers
10.5 Improve the regulation and monitoring of global financial markets and institutions and strengthen the implementation of such regulations	10.5.1 Financial Soundness Indicators
10.6 Ensure enhanced representation and voice for developing countries in decision-making in global international economic and financial institutions in order to deliver more effective, credible, accountable and legitimate institutions	10.6.1 Proportion of members and voting rights of developing countries in international organizations
10.7 Facilitate orderly, safe, regular and responsible migration and mobility of people, including through the implementation of planned and well-managed migration policies	10.7.1 Recruitment cost borne by employee as a proportion of yearly income earned in country of destination
	10.7.2 Number of countries that have implemented well-managed migration policies
10.a Implement the principle of special and differential treatment for developing countries, in particular least developed countries, in accordance with World Trade Organization agreements	10.a.1 Proportion of tariff lines applied to imports from least developed countries and developing countries with zero-tariff
10.b Encourage official development assistance and financial flows, including foreign direct investment, to States where the need is greatest, in particular least developed countries, African countries, small island developing States and landlocked	10.b.1 Total resource flows for development, by recipient and donor countries and type of flow (e.g. official development assistance, foreign direct investment and other flows)

developing countries, in accordance with their national plans and programmes	
10.c By 2030, reduce to less than 3 per cent the transaction costs of migrant remittances and eliminate remittance corridors with costs higher than 5 per cent	10.c.1 Remittance costs as a proportion of the amount remitted

Goal 11. Make cities and human settlements inclusive, safe, resilient and sustainable

11.1 By 2030, ensure access for all to adequate, safe and affordable housing and basic services and upgrade slums	11.1.1 Proportion of urban population living in slums, informal settlements or inadequate housing
11.2 By 2030, provide access to safe, affordable, accessible and sustainable transport systems for all, improving road safety, notably by expanding public transport, with special attention to the needs of those in vulnerable situations, women, children, persons with disabilities and older persons	11.2.1 Proportion of population that has convenient access to public transport, by sex, age and persons with disabilities
11.3 By 2030, enhance inclusive and sustainable urbanization and capacity for participatory, integrated and sustainable human settlement planning and management in all countries	11.3.1 Ratio of land consumption rate to population growth rate
	11.3.2 Proportion of cities with a direct participation structure of civil society in urban planning and management that operate regularly and democratically
11.4 Strengthen efforts to protect and safeguard the world's cultural and natural heritage	11.4.1 Total expenditure (public and private) per capita spent on the preservation, protection and conservation of all cultural and natural heritage, by type of heritage (cultural, natural, mixed and World Heritage Centre designation), level of government (national, regional and local/municipal), type of expenditure (operating expenditure/investment) and type of private funding (donations in kind, private non-profit sector and sponsorship)
11.5 By 2030, significantly reduce the number of deaths and the number of people affected and substantially decrease the direct economic losses relative to global gross domestic product caused by disasters, including water-related disasters, with a focus on protecting the poor and people in	11.5.1 Number of deaths, missing persons and persons affected by disaster per 100,000 people[a]
	11.5.2 Direct disaster economic loss in relation to global GDP, including disaster damage to critical infrastructure and disruption of basic services[a]

vulnerable situations	
11.6 By 2030, reduce the adverse per capita environmental impact of cities, including by paying special attention to air quality and municipal and other waste management	11.6.1 Proportion of urban solid waste regularly collected and with adequate final discharge out of total urban solid waste generated, by cities
	11.6.2 Annual mean levels of fine particulate matter (e.g. PM2.5 and PM10) in cities (population weighted)
11.7 By 2030, provide universal access to safe, inclusive and accessible, green and public spaces, in particular for women and children, older persons and persons with disabilities	11.7.1 Average share of the built-up area of cities that is open space for public use for all, by sex, age and persons with disabilities
	11.7.2 Proportion of persons victim of physical or sexual harassment, by sex, age, disability status and place of occurrence, in the previous 12 months
11.a Support positive economic, social and environmental links between urban, peri-urban and rural areas by strengthening national and regional development planning	11.a.1 Proportion of population living in cities that implement urban and regional development plans integrating population projections and resource needs, by size of city
11.b By 2020, substantially increase the number of cities and human settlements adopting and implementing integrated policies and plans towards inclusion, resource efficiency, mitigation and adaptation to climate change, resilience to disasters, and develop and implement, in line with the Sendai Framework for Disaster Risk Reduction 2015-2030, holistic disaster risk management at all levels	11.b.1 Proportion of local governments that adopt and implement local disaster risk reduction strategies in line with the Sendai Framework for Disaster Risk Reduction 2015-2030[a]
	11.b.2 Number of countries with national and local disaster risk reduction strategies[a]
11.c Support least developed countries, including through financial and technical assistance, in building sustainable and resilient buildings utilizing local materials	11.c.1 Proportion of financial support to the least developed countries that is allocated to the construction and retrofitting of sustainable, resilient and resource-efficient buildings utilizing local materials
Goal 12. Ensure sustainable consumption and production patterns	
12.1 Implement the 10-Year Framework of Programmes on Sustainable Consumption and Production Patterns, all countries taking action, with developed countries taking the lead, taking into account the development and capabilities of	12.1.1 Number of countries with sustainable consumption and production (SCP) national action plans or SCP mainstreamed as a priority or a target into national policies

developing countries	
12.2 By 2030, achieve the sustainable management and efficient use of natural resources	12.2.1 Material footprint, material footprint per capita, and material footprint per GDP
	12.2.2 Domestic material consumption, domestic material consumption per capita, and domestic material consumption per GDP
12.3 By 2030, halve per capita global food waste at the retail and consumer levels and reduce food losses along production and supply chains, including post-harvest losses	12.3.1 Global food loss index
12.4 By 2020, achieve the environmentally sound management of chemicals and all wastes throughout their life cycle, in accordance with agreed international frameworks, and significantly reduce their release to air, water and soil in order to minimize their adverse impacts on human health and the environment	12.4.1 Number of parties to international multilateral environmental agreements on hazardous waste, and other chemicals that meet their commitments and obligations in transmitting information as required by each relevant agreement
	12.4.2 Hazardous waste generated per capita, and proportion of hazardous waste treated, by type of treatment
12.5 By 2030, substantially reduce waste generation through prevention, reduction, recycling and reuse	12.5.1 National recycling rate, tons of material recycled
12.6 Encourage companies, especially large and transnational companies, to adopt sustainable practices and to integrate sustainability information into their reporting cycle	12.6.1 Number of companies publishing sustainability reports
12.7 Promote public procurement practices that are sustainable, in accordance with national policies and priorities	12.7.1 Number of countries implementing sustainable public procurement policies and action plans
12.8 By 2030, ensure that people everywhere have the relevant information and awareness for sustainable development and lifestyles in harmony with nature	12.8.1 Extent to which (i) global citizenship education and (ii) education for sustainable development (including climate change education) are mainstreamed in (a) national education policies; (b) curricula; (c) teacher education; and (d) student assessment
12.a Support developing countries to strengthen their scientific and technological capacity to move	12.a.1 Amount of support to developing countries on research and development for sustainable

towards more sustainable patterns of consumption and production	consumption and production and environmentally sound technologies
12.b Develop and implement tools to monitor sustainable development impacts for sustainable tourism that creates jobs and promotes local culture and products	12.b.1 Number of sustainable tourism strategies or policies and implemented action plans with agreed monitoring and evaluation tools
12.c Rationalize inefficient fossil-fuel subsidies that encourage wasteful consumption by removing market distortions, in accordance with national circumstances, including by restructuring taxation and phasing out those harmful subsidies, where they exist, to reflect their environmental impacts, taking fully into account the specific needs and conditions of developing countries and minimizing the possible adverse impacts on their development in a manner that protects the poor and the affected communities	12.c.1 Amount of fossil-fuel subsidies per unit of GDP (production and consumption) and as a proportion of total national expenditure on fossil fuels
Goal 13. Take urgent action to combat climate change and its impacts	
13.1 Strengthen resilience and adaptive capacity to climate-related hazards and natural disasters in all countries	13.1.1 Number of countries with national and local disaster risk reduction strategies[a]
	13.1.2 Number of deaths, missing persons and persons affected by disaster per 100,000 people[a]
13.2 Integrate climate change measures into national policies, strategies and planning	13.2.1 Number of countries that have communicated the establishment or operationalization of an integrated policy/strategy/plan which increases their ability to adapt to the adverse impacts of climate change, and foster climate resilience and low greenhouse gas emissions development in a manner that does not threaten food production (including a national adaptation plan, nationally determined contribution, national communication, biennial update report or other)
13.3 Improve education, awareness-raising and human and institutional capacity on climate change mitigation, adaptation, impact reduction and early warning	13.3.1 Number of countries that have integrated mitigation, adaptation, impact reduction and early warning into primary, secondary and tertiary curricula
	13.3.2 Number of countries that have communicated the

	strengthening of institutional, systemic and individual capacity-building to implement adaptation, mitigation and technology transfer, and development actions
13.a Implement the commitment undertaken by developed-country parties to the United Nations Framework Convention on Climate Change to a goal of mobilizing jointly $100 billion annually by 2020 from all sources to address the needs of developing countries in the context of meaningful mitigation actions and transparency on implementation and fully operationalize the Green Climate Fund through its capitalization as soon as possible	13.a.1 Mobilizedamount of United States dollars per year starting in 2020 accountable towards the $100 billion commitment
13.b Promote mechanisms for raising capacity for effective climate change-related planning and management in least developed countries and small island developing States, including focusing on women, youth and local and marginalized communities	13.b.1 Number of least developed countries and small island developing States that are receiving specialized support, and amount of support, including finance, technology and capacity-building, for mechanisms for raising capacities for effective climate change-related planning and management, including focusing on women, youth and local and marginalized communities

Goal 14. Conserve and sustainably use the oceans, seas and marine resources for sustainable development

14.1 By 2025, prevent and significantly reduce marine pollution of all kinds, in particular from land-based activities, including marine debris and nutrient pollution	14.1.1 Index of coastal eutrophication and floating plastic debris density
14.2 By 2020, sustainably manage and protect marine and coastal ecosystems to avoid significant adverse impacts, including by strengthening their resilience, and take action for their restoration in order to achieve healthy and productive oceans	14.2.1 Proportion of national exclusive economic zones managed using ecosystem-based approaches
14.3 Minimize and address the impacts of ocean acidification, including through enhanced scientific cooperation at all levels	14.3.1 Average marine acidity (pH) measured at agreed suite of representative sampling stations
14.4 By 2020, effectively regulate harvesting and end overfishing, illegal,	14.4.1 Proportion of fish stocks within biologically sustainable

unreported and unregulated fishing and destructive fishing practices and implement science-based management plans, in order to restore fish stocks in the shortest time feasible, at least to levels that can produce maximum sustainable yield as determined by their biological characteristics	levels
14.5 By 2020, conserve at least 10 per cent of coastal and marine areas, consistent with national and international law and based on the best available scientific information	14.5.1 Coverage of protected areas in relation to marine areas
14.6 By 2020, prohibit certain forms of fisheries subsidies which contribute to overcapacity and overfishing, eliminate subsidies that contribute to illegal, unreported and unregulated fishing and refrain from introducing new such subsidies, recognizing that appropriate and effective special and differential treatment for developing and least developed countries should be an integral part of the World Trade Organization fisheries subsidies negotiation[c]	14.6.1 Progress by countries in the degree of implementation of international instruments aiming to combat illegal, unreported and unregulated fishing
14.7 By 2030, increase the economic benefits to small island developing States and least developed countries from the sustainable use of marine resources, including through sustainable management of fisheries, aquaculture and tourism	14.7.1 Sustainable fisheries as a percentage of GDP in small island developing States, least developed countries and all countries
14.a Increase scientific knowledge, develop research capacity and transfer marine technology, taking into account the Intergovernmental Oceanographic Commission Criteria and Guidelines on the Transfer of Marine Technology, in order to improve ocean health and to enhance the contribution of marine biodiversity to the development of developing countries, in particular small island developing States and least developed countries	14.a.1 Proportion of total research budget allocated to research in the field of marine technology
14.b Provide access for small-scale artisanal fishers to marine resources and markets	14.b.1 Progress by countries in the degree of application of a legal/regulatory/policy/institutional framework which recognizes and protects access rights for small-

	scale fisheries
14.c Enhance the conservation and sustainable use of oceans and their resources by implementing international law as reflected in the United Nations Convention on the Law of the Sea, which provides the legal framework for the conservation and sustainable use of oceans and their resources, as recalled in paragraph 158 of "The future we want"	14.c.1 Number of countries making progress in ratifying, accepting and implementing through legal, policy and institutional frameworks, ocean-related instruments that implement international law, as reflected in the United Nation Convention on the Law of the Sea, for the conservation and sustainable use of the oceans and their resources

Goal 15. Protect, restore and promote sustainable use of terrestrial ecosystems, sustainably manage forests, combat desertification, and halt and reverse land degradation and halt biodiversity loss

15.1 By 2020, ensure the conservation, restoration and sustainable use of terrestrial and inland freshwater ecosystems and their services, in particular forests, wetlands, mountains and drylands, in line with obligations under international agreements	15.1.1 Forest area as a proportion of total land area
	15.1.2 Proportion of important sites for terrestrial and freshwater biodiversity that are covered by protected areas, by ecosystem type
15.2 By 2020, promote the implementation of sustainable management of all types of forests, halt deforestation, restore degraded forests and substantially increase afforestation and reforestation globally	15.2.1 Progress towards sustainable forest management
15.3 By 2030, combat desertification, restore degraded land and soil, including land affected by desertification, drought and floods, and strive to achieve a land degradation-neutral world	15.3.1 Proportion of land that is degraded over total land area
15.4 By 2030, ensure the conservation of mountain ecosystems, including their biodiversity, in order to enhance their capacity to provide benefits that are essential for sustainable development	15.4.1 Coverage by protected areas of important sites for mountain biodiversity
	15.4.2 Mountain Green Cover Index
15.5 Take urgent and significant action to reduce the degradation of natural habitats, halt the loss of biodiversity and, by 2020, protect and prevent the extinction of threatened species	15.5.1 Red List Index
15.6 Promote fair and equitable sharing of the benefits arising from the utilization of genetic resources and promote appropriate access to such resources, as internationally agreed	15.6.1 Number of countries that have adopted legislative, administrative and policy frameworks to ensure fair and equitable sharing of benefits

15.7 Take urgent action to end poaching and trafficking of protected species of flora and fauna and address both demand and supply of illegal wildlife products	15.7.1 Proportion of traded wildlife that was poached or illicitly trafficked
15.8 By 2020, introduce measures to prevent the introduction and significantly reduce the impact of invasive alien species on land and water ecosystems and control or eradicate the priority species	15.8.1 Proportion of countries adopting relevant national legislation and adequately resourcing the prevention or control of invasive alien species
15.9 By 2020, integrate ecosystem and biodiversity values into national and local planning, development processes, poverty reduction strategies and accounts	15.9.1 Progress towards national targets established in accordance with Aichi Biodiversity Target 2 of the Strategic Plan for Biodiversity 2011-2020
15.a Mobilize and significantly increase financial resources from all sources to conserve and sustainably use biodiversity and ecosystems	15.a.1 Official development assistance and public expenditure on conservation and sustainable use of biodiversity and ecosystems
15.b Mobilize significant resources from all sources and at all levels to finance sustainable forest management and provide adequate incentives to developing countries to advance such management, including for conservation and reforestation	15.b.1 Official development assistance and public expenditure on conservation and sustainable use of biodiversity and ecosystems
15.c Enhance global support for efforts to combat poaching and trafficking of protected species, including by increasing the capacity of local communities to pursue sustainable livelihood opportunities	15.c.1 Proportion of traded wildlife that was poached or illicitly trafficked
Goal 16. Promote peaceful and inclusive societies for sustainable development, provide access to justice for all and build effective, accountable and inclusive institutions at all levels	
16.1 Significantly reduce all forms of violence and related death rates everywhere	16.1.1 Number of victims of intentional homicide per 100,000 population, by sex and age
	16.1.2 Conflict-related deaths per 100,000 population, by sex, age and cause
	16.1.3 Proportion of population subjected to physical, psychological or sexual violence in the previous 12 months
	16.1.4 Proportion of population that feel safe walking alone around the area they live
16.2 End abuse, exploitation,	16.2.1 Proportion of children aged

trafficking and all forms of violence against and torture of children	1-17 years who experienced any physical punishment and/or psychological aggression by caregivers in the past month
	16.2.2 Number of victims of human trafficking per 100,000 population, by sex, age and form of exploitation
	16.2.3 Proportion of young women and men aged 18-29 years who experienced sexual violence by age 18
16.3 Promote the rule of law at the national and international levels and ensure equal access to justice for all	16.3.1 Proportion of victims of violence in the previous 12 months who reported their victimization to competent authorities or other officially recognized conflict resolution mechanisms
	16.3.2 Unsentenced detainees as a proportion of overall prison population
16.4 By 2030, significantly reduce illicit financial and arms flows, strengthen the recovery and return of stolen assets and combat all forms of organized crime	16.4.1 Total value of inward and outward illicit financial flows (in current United States dollars)
	16.4.2 Proportion of seized small arms and light weapons that are recorded and traced, in accordance with international standards and legal instruments
16.5 Substantially reduce corruption and bribery in all their forms	16.5.1 Proportion of persons who had at least one contact with a public official and who paid a bribe to a public official, or were asked for a bribe by those public officials, during the previous 12 months
	16.5.2 Proportion of businesses that had at least one contact with a public official and that paid a bribe to a public official, or were asked for a bribe by those public officials during the previous 12 months
16.6 Develop effective, accountable and transparent institutions at all levels	16.6.1 Primary government expenditures as a proportion of original approved budget, by sector (or by budget codes or similar)
	16.6.2 Proportion of the population satisfied with their last experience of public services
16.7 Ensure responsive, inclusive, participatory and representative decision-making at all levels	16.7.1 Proportions of positions (by sex, age, persons with disabilities and population groups) in public

	institutions (national and local legislatures, public service, and judiciary) compared to national distributions
	16.7.2 Proportion of population who believe decision-making is inclusive and responsive, by sex, age, disability and population group
16.8 Broaden and strengthen the participation of developing countries in the institutions of global governance	16.8.1 Proportion of members and voting rights of developing countries in international organizations
16.9 By 2030, provide legal identity for all, including birth registration	16.9.1 Proportion of children under 5 years of age whose births have been registered with a civil authority, by age
16.10 Ensure public access to information and protect fundamental freedoms, in accordance with national legislation and international agreements	16.10.1 Number of verified cases of killing, kidnapping, enforced disappearance, arbitrary detention and torture of journalists, associated media personnel, trade unionists and human rights advocates in the previous 12 months
	16.10.2 Number of countries that adopt and implement constitutional, statutory and/or policy guarantees for public access to information
16.a Strengthen relevant national institutions, including through international cooperation, for building capacity at all levels, in particular in developing countries, to prevent violence and combat terrorism and crime	16.a.1 Existence of independent national human rights institutions in compliance with the Paris Principles
16.b Promote and enforce non-discriminatory laws and policies for sustainable development	16.b.1 Proportion of population reporting having personally felt discriminated against or harassed in the previous 12 months on the basis of a ground of discrimination prohibited under international human rights law

Goal 17. Strengthen the means of implementation and revitalize the Global Partnership for Sustainable Development

Finance	
17.1 Strengthen domestic resource mobilization, including through international support to developing countries, to improve domestic capacity for tax and other revenue collection	17.1.1 Total government revenue as a proportion of GDP, by source
	17.1.2 Proportion of domestic budget funded by domestic taxes

17.2 Developed countries to implement fully their official development assistance commitments, including the commitment by many developed countries to achieve the target of 0.7 per cent of gross national income for official development assistance (ODA/GNI) to developing countries and 0.15 to 0.20 per cent of ODA/GNI to least developed countries; ODA providers are encouraged to consider setting a target to provide at least 0.20 per cent of ODA/GNI to least developed countries	17.2.1 Net official development assistance, total and to least developed countries, as a proportion of the Organization for Economic Cooperation and Development (OECD) Development Assistance Committee donors' gross national income (GNI)
17.3 Mobilize additional financial resources for developing countries from multiple sources	17.3.1 Foreign direct investments (FDI), official development assistance and South-South Cooperation as a proportion of total domestic budget
	17.3.2 Volume of remittances (in United States dollars) as a proportion of total GDP
17.4 Assist developing countries in attaining long-term debt sustainability through coordinated policies aimed at fostering debt financing, debt relief and debt restructuring, as appropriate, and address the external debt of highly indebted poor countries to reduce debt distress	17.4.1 Debt service as a proportion of exports of goods and services
17.5 Adopt and implement investment promotion regimes for least developed countries	17.5.1 Number of countries that adopt and implement investment promotion regimes for least developed countries
Technology	
17.6 Enhance North-South, South-South and triangular regional and international cooperation on and access to science, technology and innovation and enhance knowledge-sharing on mutually agreed terms, including through improved coordination among existing mechanisms, in particular at the United Nations level, and through a global technology facilitation mechanism	17.6.1 Number of science and/or technology cooperation agreements and programmes between countries, by type of cooperation
	17.6.2 Fixed Internet broadband subscriptions per 100 inhabitants, by speed
17.7 Promote the development, transfer, dissemination and diffusion of environmentally sound technologies to developing countries on favourable	17.7.1 Total amount of approved funding for developing countries to promote the development, transfer, dissemination and diffusion of

terms, including on concessional and preferential terms, as mutually agreed	environmentally sound technologies
17.8 Fully operationalize the technology bank and science, technology and innovation capacity-building mechanism for least developed countries by 2017 and enhance the use of enabling technology, in particular information and communications technology	17.8.1 Proportion of individuals using the Internet
Capacity-building	
17.9 Enhance international support for implementing effective and targeted capacity-building in developing countries to support national plans to implement all the Sustainable Development Goals, including through North-South, South-South and triangular cooperation	17.9.1 Dollar value of financial and technical assistance (including through North-South, South-South and triangular cooperation) committed to developing countries
Trade	
17.10 Promote a universal, rules-based, open, non-discriminatory and equitable multilateral trading system under the World Trade Organization, including through the conclusion of negotiations under its Doha Development Agenda	17.10.1 Worldwide weighted tariff-average
17.11 Significantly increase the exports of developing countries, in particular with a view to doubling the least developed countries' share of global exports by 2020	17.11.1 Developing countries' and least developed countries' share of global exports
17.12 Realize timely implementation of duty-free and quota-free market access on a lasting basis for all least developed countries, consistent with World Trade Organization decisions, including by ensuring that preferential rules of origin applicable to imports from least developed countries are transparent and simple, and contribute to facilitating market access	17.12.1 Average tariffs faced by developing countries, least developed countries and small island developing States
Systemic issues	
Policy and institutional coherence	
17.13 Enhance global macroeconomic stability, including through policy coordination and policy coherence	17.13.1 Macroeconomic Dashboard
17.14 Enhance policy coherence for sustainable development	17.14.1 Number of countries with mechanisms in place to enhance policy coherence of sustainable

	development
17.15 Respect each country's policy space and leadership to establish and implement policies for poverty eradication and sustainable development	17.15.1 Extent of use of country-owned results frameworks and planning tools by providers of development cooperation
Multi-stakeholder partnerships	
17.16 Enhance the Global Partnership for Sustainable Development, complemented by multi-stakeholder partnerships that mobilize and share knowledge, expertise, technology and financial resources, to support the achievement of the Sustainable Development Goals in all countries, in particular developing countries	17.16.1 Number of countries reporting progress in multi-stakeholder development effectiveness monitoring frameworks that support the achievement of the sustainable development goals
17.17 Encourage and promote effective public, public-private and civil society partnerships, building on the experience and resourcing strategies of partnerships	17.17.1 Amount of United States dollars committed to public-private and civil society partnerships
Data, monitoring and accountability	
17.18 By 2020, enhance capacity-building support to developing countries, including for least developed countries and small island developing States, to increase significantly the availability of high-quality, timely and reliable data disaggregated by income, gender, age, race, ethnicity, migratory status, disability, geographic location and other characteristics relevant in national contexts	17.18.1 Proportion of sustainable development indicators produced at the national level with full disaggregation when relevant to the target, in accordance with the Fundamental Principles of Official Statistics
	17.18.2 Number of countries that have national statistical legislation that complies with the Fundamental Principles of Official Statistics
	17.18.3 Number of countries with a national statistical plan that is fully funded and under implementation, by source of funding
17.19 By 2030, build on existing initiatives to develop measurements of progress on sustainable development that complement gross domestic product, and support statistical capacity-building in developing countries	17.19.1 Dollar value of all resources made available to strengthen statistical capacity in developing countries
	17.19.2 Proportion of countries that (a) have conducted at least one population and housing census in the last 10 years; and (b) have achieved 100 per cent birth registration and 80 per cent death registration

Chapter Highlights

- The SDGs are a set of global ambitions established by the United Nations to address issues like poverty, hunger, health, education, climate change, gender equality, and environmental sustainability by 2030.
- The process began in 2012 with the UN Conference on Sustainable Development (Rio+20), which mandated the creation of a set of sustainable development goals.
- The SDGs are integrated, interconnected, universal, and ambitious, setting specific, measurable targets for 2030.
- No Poverty - Eradicate extreme poverty, provide social protection, ensure equal access to resources, and address unemployment and inequality.
- Zero Hunger - End hunger, achieve food security, improve nutrition, and promote sustainable agriculture.
- Good Health and Well-being - Ensure healthy lives and promote well-being for all at all ages, including universal healthcare, improved maternal health, and combating epidemics.
- Quality Education - Ensure inclusive, equitable quality education and promote lifelong learning opportunities for all.
- Gender Equality - Achieve gender equality and empower all women and girls by ending discrimination and violence, ensuring leadership opportunities, and equal access to education and resources.
- Clean Water and Sanitation - Ensure access to clean water and sanitation for all and promote sustainable water management.
- Affordable and Clean Energy - Ensure access to affordable, reliable, sustainable, and modern energy for all, with a focus on renewable energy and energy efficiency.
- Decent Work and Economic Growth - Promote sustained, inclusive economic growth, full and productive employment, and decent work for all.
- Industry, Innovation, and Infrastructure - Build resilient infrastructure, promote sustainable industrialization, and foster innovation.
- Reduced Inequalities - Reduce inequalities within and among countries by promoting social, economic, and political inclusion.

- Sustainable Cities and Communities - Make cities and communities inclusive, safe, resilient, and sustainable, ensuring affordable housing, sustainable urbanization, and green public spaces.
- Responsible Consumption and Production - Ensure sustainable consumption and production patterns, reduce waste generation, and promote resource efficiency.
- Climate Action - Take urgent action to combat climate change and its effects, promoting resilience, reducing greenhouse gas emissions, and integrating climate measures into policies.
- Life Below Water - Conserve and sustainably use oceans, seas, and marine resources, including reducing marine pollution and protecting marine biodiversity.
- Life on Land - Protect, restore, and promote sustainable use of terrestrial ecosystems, combat desertification, and halt biodiversity loss.
- Peace, Justice, and Strong Institutions - Promote peaceful, inclusive societies, ensure access to justice for all, and build effective, accountable institutions.
- Partnerships for the Goals - Strengthen global partnerships for sustainable development, increase financial support, foster technology transfer, and promote global collaboration.

Empowerment and Future Scope of the SDGs

4.1 How to Contribute to Achieving the SDGs

Simple Ways to Help Achieve the SDGs

- **Learn About the SDGs:** Take some time to understand what the SDGs are and why they matter. Learning about each goal helps you see how they relate to our everyday lives and the world around us.

- **Adopt Small Daily Actions**
  - **Save Water:** You can save water by turning off the tap while brushing your teeth or taking shorter showers.
  - **Reduce Waste:** Try to use less plastic by bringing reusable bags when shopping and using containers that can be washed and reused. Composting food scraps is another great way to cut down on waste.
  - **Energy Conservation:** Remember to turn off lights when you leave a room, and consider using energy-saving light bulbs and appliances to reduce energy consumption.

- **Support Eco-Friendly Products:** Choose products that are made from sustainable materials or are environmentally friendly. By buying from companies that care about the planet, you help promote better practices in business.

- **Volunteer Your Time:** Get involved in local community projects or organizations that focus on sustainability and social issues. Volunteering can include activities like cleaning up parks, helping in community gardens, or supporting educational programs for young people.

- **Educate Others:** Share what you learn about the SDGs with your friends and family. Talking about these goals can inspire others to think about their own actions and how they can help.

- **Advocate for Change:** Speak up about important issues in your community. Attend local meetings or write to your representatives about policies that support sustainability and social justice.

- **Make Informed Choices:** When shopping, think about where products come from and how they are made. Supporting fair trade products ensures that workers are treated fairly and paid well.

- **Participate in Local Initiatives:** Join local efforts like tree planting events or community clean-ups. These activities help improve your environment and contribute directly to goals related to climate action and sustainability.
- **Donate to Relevant Causes:**If you can, consider donating money or resources to organizations that work towards achieving specific SDGs, such as those focused on education, health, or environmental protection.
- **Stay Informed and Engaged:**Keep learning about sustainability issues and participate in campaigns or movements that align with your values. Staying engaged helps keep important topics alive in your community.

Table 4.1 provides a comprehensive guide on simple actions that can be taken for sustainable development.By taking these simple steps, everyone can play a part in achieving the SDGs. Small changes in our daily lives can lead to big improvements for our planet and society by 2030.

Table 4.1: Everyday Steps to Achieve the SDGs.

Action	Description	SDG Relevance
Learn	Understand the SDGs and their importance. Explore how they relate to your life and the world.	All SDGs
Daily Actions	- Save Water: Turn off taps, take shorter showers. - Reduce Waste: Use reusable bags, containers; compost food scraps. - Conserve Energy: Use energy-efficient appliances.	SDG 6 (Clean Water and Sanitation), SDG 12 (Responsible Consumption and Production), SDG 13 (Climate Action)
Support Eco-Friendly Products	Choose products made sustainably or from eco-friendly sources. Support businesses with environmental and social responsibility.	SDG 12 (Responsible Consumption and Production), SDG 15 (Life on Land)
Volunteer	Participate in community projects related to sustainability and social issues (e.g., park cleanups, community gardens, educational programs).	All SDGs
Educate Others	Share your knowledge about the SDGs with friends and family to inspire action.	SDG 4 (Quality Education), SDG 17 (Partnerships for the Goals)
Advocate for	Speak up about important	All SDGs

Change	issues. Attend local meetings and contact representatives to support policies that promote sustainability and social justice.	
Make Informed Choices	Consider the source and production methods of products. Support fair trade to ensure fair treatment and wages for workers.	SDG 8 (Decent Work and Economic Growth), SDG 12 (Responsible Consumption and Production)
Participate in Local Initiatives	Join tree-planting events, community cleanups, and other local efforts.	SDG 11 (Sustainable Cities and Communities), SDG 13 (Climate Action), SDG 15 (Life on Land)
Donate	Contribute to organizations working towards specific SDGs (e.g., education, health, environmental protection).	All SDGs
Stay Informed and Engaged	Continuously learn about sustainability issues and participate in relevant campaigns and movements.	All SDGs

4.2 The Role of People, Companies, and Governments

Sustainable development requires a multi-faceted approach involving individuals, businesses, and governments.

- Individuals play a crucial role in promoting sustainability by actively participating in their communities, raising awareness about social and environmental issues, adopting sustainable lifestyles, supporting local economies, and participating in grassroots movements. They can join local organizations, volunteer, and participate in community initiatives, advocating for change through actions like writing letters to officials and organizing discussions.

- Companies can contribute to sustainability by implementing sustainable practices, promoting eco-friendly products, fostering corporate social responsibility, building trust through transparency, and collaborating with other businesses. These practices reduce waste, conserve energy, and source materials responsibly, improving operational efficiency and reducing costs. By engaging in community initiatives, supporting education programs, and funding environmental conservation projects, companies can attract environmentally conscious consumers and enhance their brand reputation.

- Governments play a crucial role in promoting sustainable development by creating supportive policies, investing in public services, fostering community engagement, supporting innovation, and enforcing environmental regulations. These policies encourage renewable energy, pollution reduction, and sustainable practices. They also invest in education, healthcare, and infrastructure to improve community well-being. Community participation in decision-making processes is also encouraged through town halls and forums. These measures drive economic growth and environmental protection.

Thus, by working together, individuals, businesses, and governments can create a more sustainable future. This collaborative effort will lead to stronger, more resilient communities, reduced environmental impact, increased consumer trust, and improved public health. **Table 4.1** briefs the importance of collaboration in driving sustainability and positive change, highlighting the responsibilities and impacts of individuals, companies, and governments, strategies for sustainable development, shared efforts towards community, environmental, and economic progress, and stakeholder roles.

4.2.1 The Role of Individuals

Individuals can be powerful agents of change in their communities. Here are ways they can make a difference:

1. **Get Involved Locally:** Join community organizations or initiatives that focus on local issues. This could include volunteering at shelters, participating in clean-up drives, or supporting local arts and culture.

2. **Educate and Advocate:** Share knowledge about important social and environmental issues with friends and family. Advocacy can take many forms, such as writing letters to local representatives or organizing community discussions.

3. **Practice Sustainable Living:** Adopt eco-friendly habits like reducing waste, conserving water, and using public transportation. Small personal changes can inspire others to follow suit.

4. **Support Local Businesses:** Choose to shop at local stores or farmers' markets instead of large chains. Supporting local economies helps build stronger communities.

5. **Engage in Grassroots Activism:** Participate in or organize grassroots movements that address community needs. This can involve protests, awareness campaigns, or lobbying for policy changes.

4.2.2 The Role of Companies

Businesses have a significant impact on both the economy and the environment. Here's how they can grow while being environmentally responsible:

1. **Implement Sustainable Practices:** Companies can adopt sustainable practices by reducing waste, conserving energy, and sourcing materials responsibly. This not only helps the environment but can also reduce operational costs.
2. **Innovate Eco-Friendly Products:** Develop products that are environmentally friendly or made from sustainable materials. This attracts customers who prioritize sustainability.
3. **Corporate Social Responsibility (CSR):** Engage in CSR initiatives that benefit the community and environment. This could include sponsoring local events, supporting education programs, or funding environmental conservation projects.
4. **Transparency and Reporting:** Be transparent about business practices and environmental impacts. Regularly report on sustainability goals and progress to build trust with consumers.
5. **Collaborate with Other Businesses:** Partner with other companies to share resources and knowledge about sustainability practices. Collaborative efforts can lead to more significant impacts than working alone.

4.2.4 The Role of Governments

Governments play a crucial role in facilitating large-scale changes through policy-making and regulation:

1. **Create Supportive Policies:** Implement policies that promote sustainable development, such as incentives for renewable energy use or regulations that limit pollution.
2. **Invest in Public Services:** Allocate funds towards public services that enhance community well-being, such as education, healthcare, and infrastructure improvements.
3. **Encourage Community Engagement:** Foster an environment where citizens can participate in decision-making processes through town halls or public forums.

4. **Support Innovation:** Invest in research and development for sustainable technologies and practices that can drive economic growth while protecting the environment.
5. **Strengthen Environmental Regulations:** Enforce laws that protect natural resources and ensure businesses comply with environmental standards to safeguard public health.

By working together—individuals taking action in their communities, businesses adopting sustainable practices, and governments creating supportive policies—society can achieve significant positive changes that benefit everyone now and in the future.

Table 4.1: Key Responsibilities and Impacts of Individuals, Companies, and Governments.

Role	Key Actions	Impact of Actions
Individuals		
Get Involved Locally	- Join community organizations or initiatives focused on local issues (e.g., volunteering at shelters, participating in clean-up drives, or supporting arts and culture).	- Builds stronger and more resilient communities.
Educate and Advocate	- Share knowledge about social and environmental issues with friends and family. - Engage in advocacy (e.g., writing to local representatives, organizing community discussions).	- Raises awareness and drives collective action for change.
Practice Sustainable Living	- Adopt eco-friendly habits like reducing waste, conserving water, and using public transportation. - Encourage others to follow suit by leading by example.	- Reduces environmental footprint and inspires broader adoption of sustainable habits.
Support Local Businesses	- Choose to shop at local stores or farmers' markets instead of large chains to strengthen local economies.	- Strengthens local economies and promotes self-sufficiency within communities.
Engage in Grassroots Activism	- Participate in or organize grassroots movements addressing community needs (e.g., protests, awareness	- Drives policy changes and increases community engagement in solving

	campaigns, or lobbying for policy changes).	local issues.
Companies		
Implement Sustainable Practices	- Adopt sustainable practices by reducing waste, conserving energy, and sourcing materials responsibly. - Achieve both environmental benefits and cost savings.	- Minimizes environmental impact and enhances long-term business profitability.
Innovate Eco-Friendly Products	- Develop and market environmentally friendly products made from sustainable materials to attract eco-conscious consumers.	- Meets consumer demand for sustainability and boosts brand loyalty.
Corporate Social Responsibility (CSR)	- Engage in CSR activities (e.g., sponsoring local events, supporting education programs, or funding environmental conservation initiatives).	- Builds goodwill, improves community relations, and enhances the company's public image.
Transparency and Reporting	- Regularly report on business practices, sustainability goals, and progress to build trust with consumers.	- Increases consumer trust and strengthens brand reputation.
Collaborate with Other Businesses	- Partner with other companies to share resources and knowledge about sustainability practices, leading to greater collective impact.	- Encourages innovation and amplifies positive environmental and social outcomes.
Governments		
Create Supportive Policies	- Enact policies promoting sustainable development (e.g., renewable energy incentives, pollution control regulations).	- Accelerates the adoption of sustainable practices across society.
Invest in Public Services	- Allocate resources to improve education, healthcare, and infrastructure for community well-being.	- Enhances quality of life and supports long-term socio-economic growth.
Encourage Community Engagement	- Facilitate citizen participation in decision-making through town halls or public forums.	- Strengthens democratic governance and ensures policies reflect community needs.
Support	- Fund research and	- Drives economic

| Innovation | development of sustainable technologies and practices to promote economic growth while protecting the environment. | advancement and promotes environmentally friendly technological breakthroughs. |
| Strengthen Environmental Regulations | - Enforce environmental laws that protect natural resources and ensure businesses comply with standards to safeguard public health. | - Safeguards natural resources and improves public health and environmental quality. |

4.3 Working Together Locally and Globally

Communities, countries, and organizations can work together effectively to meet the Sustainable Development Goals (SDGs) both locally and globally. Following sections detail that how they (communities, countries, and organizations) can start local projects, emphasize teamwork between nations, and share successful ideas.

4.3.1 How Communities Can Start Local Projects to Meet SDG Goals

1. **Identify Local Needs**: Communities should begin by assessing their specific needs and challenges. This can involve surveys, community meetings, or discussions with local leaders to understand which SDGs are most relevant.
2. **Engage Community Members**: Involve residents in the planning process. This can be done through workshops or brainstorming sessions where everyone can contribute ideas and solutions.
3. **Form Partnerships**: Collaborate with local schools, businesses, non-profits, and government agencies. These partnerships can provide resources, expertise, and support for projects aimed at achieving the SDGs.
4. **Develop Action Plans**: Create clear action plans that outline goals, timelines, and responsibilities for each project. Setting measurable objectives helps track progress and maintain motivation.
5. **Implement Projects**: Start with small-scale initiatives like community gardens, recycling programs, or educational workshops on sustainability. These projects can serve as models for larger efforts in the future.

6. **Monitor and Evaluate**: Regularly assess the impact of the projects to see what works and what doesn't. Gathering feedback from participants helps refine future initiatives.

7. **Share Success Stories**: Celebrate achievements within the community to inspire others and attract more participants for future projects.

4.3.2 The Importance of Teamwork Between Countries

1. **Addressing Global Challenges**: Many issues like climate change, poverty, and health crises transcend national borders. Collaborative efforts are essential to tackle these global challenges effectively.

2. **Sharing Resources and Knowledge**: Countries can benefit from sharing best practices, technologies, and research findings. This exchange of information can lead to innovative solutions that might not be possible in isolation.

3. **Strengthening Global Partnerships**: International agreements and partnerships foster cooperation among nations. Initiatives like the Paris Agreement on climate change exemplify how countries can work together toward common goals.

4. **Building Capacity**: Developed nations can assist developing countries by providing financial aid, training, and resources needed to implement SDG-related projects effectively.

5. **Promoting Peaceful Collaboration**: Teamwork between countries encourages dialogue and understanding, which are crucial for maintaining peace and stability while working toward shared objectives.

By working together at local and global levels, communities can effectively address challenges while contributing to the achievement of the SDGs. Collaboration enhances the potential for success by pooling resources, sharing knowledge, and inspiring collective action toward a sustainable future.

4.3.3 Sharing Ideas and Successful Methods

1. **Create Platforms for Exchange**: Establish online platforms or forums where communities and organizations can share their experiences, successes, and challenges related to SDG projects.

2. **Host Conferences and Workshops**: Organize events that bring together stakeholders from different regions to discuss strategies, share success stories, and collaborate on new initiatives.
3. **Utilize Social Media**: Leverage social media to highlight successful projects and innovative ideas from various communities worldwide. This visibility can inspire others to adopt similar approaches.
4. **Document Case Studies**: Compile case studies of successful local projects that align with the SDGs. These documents can serve as valuable resources for others looking to implement similar initiatives.
5. **Encourage Student Involvement**: Engage students in global projects focused on the SDGs through schools or universities. Programs that connect students from different countries can foster a sense of global citizenship while sharing knowledge and creative solutions.

4.4 What's Next for the SDGs

As we approach the 2030 deadline for achieving the Sustainable Development Goals (SDGs), several factors could influence progress. Following is an overview of the challenges, potential changes to the goals, and the importance of working efficiently to meet targets.

4.4.1 Challenges That Might Slow Down Progress by 2030

1. **Economic Disparities**: Widespread poverty and inequality continue to hinder efforts to achieve the SDGs. Many regions, particularly in sub-Saharan Africa and South Asia, face significant challenges due to economic instability and lack of resources.
2. **Climate Change**: The impacts of climate change threaten to reverse progress made in various areas, including health, food security, and water access. Extreme weather events can disrupt local economies and exacerbate existing vulnerabilities.
3. **Political Instability**: Conflicts and political unrest in several countries can derail development efforts. War and violence lead to humanitarian crises that divert attention and resources away from sustainable development initiatives.

4. **Lack of Coordination**: Effective implementation of the SDGs requires coordinated efforts among governments, businesses, and civil society. A lack of collaboration can result in fragmented approaches that fail to address the interconnected nature of the goals.

5. **Data Collection Issues**: Measuring progress toward the SDGs relies on accurate data collection. In many regions, especially in developing countries, insufficient data hampers the ability to track advancements and identify areas needing attention.

4.4.2 How the Goals Could Change to Fit Future Needs

1. **Adaptation to Emerging Challenges**: As new global challenges arise, such as pandemics or technological disruptions, the SDGs may need revisions to address these issues effectively. This could involve adding new targets or adjusting existing ones.

2. **Focus on Inclusivity**: Future iterations of the SDGs might place greater emphasis on inclusivity, ensuring that marginalized communities have a voice in decision-making processes and benefit from development initiatives.

3. **Integration of Technology**: Incorporating advancements in technology could enhance efforts to achieve the SDGs. This may include leveraging digital tools for education, healthcare, and environmental monitoring.

4. **Greater Emphasis on Resilience**: Future goals may prioritize building resilience against shocks like climate change or economic downturns, ensuring that communities can adapt and recover from crises.

4.4.3 The Importance of Working Faster and Smarter to Meet Targets

1. **Urgency of Action**: With only a few years left until 2030, it is crucial for all stakeholders—governments, businesses, and individuals—to accelerate their efforts. Delayed actions can lead to missed opportunities for progress.

2. **Efficiency in Resource Use**: Working smarter means optimizing resource allocation and utilizing innovative solutions that maximize impact while minimizing waste. This includes adopting sustainable practices in business operations and community projects.

3. **Collaboration Across Sectors**: Enhanced collaboration between public and private sectors can lead to more effective strategies for achieving the SDGs. Sharing knowledge and resources can help overcome common challenges more efficiently.

4. **Monitoring Progress**: Establishing robust mechanisms for tracking progress allows for timely adjustments to strategies as needed. Regular assessments help ensure that initiatives remain aligned with evolving needs and challenges.

5. **Engagement of Youth and Communities**: Mobilizing young people and local communities is essential for driving change at all levels. Their involvement brings fresh perspectives and innovative ideas that can help accelerate progress toward the SDGs.

By addressing these challenges head-on, adapting goals as necessary, and committing to faster, smarter actions, stakeholders can work together effectively to achieve the Sustainable Development Goals by 2030, creating a more equitable and sustainable world for all.

4.5 New Ideas for a Sustainable Future

To create a sustainable future, innovative technologies and practices play a crucial role. Following sections provide an overview of how new inventions like solar panels and electric cars, recycling efforts, and the rise of green jobs contribute to protecting the planet.

4.5.1 Using New Inventions to Protect the Planet

1. **Solar Panels**: Solar panels convert sunlight into electricity, providing a renewable energy source that reduces reliance on fossil fuels. As technology advances, solar panels are becoming more efficient and versatile, such as being integrated into electric vehicles (EVs). This integration allows cars to harness solar energy, extending their range and reducing the need for traditional charging stations.

2. **Electric Cars**: Electric vehicles are key to reducing greenhouse gas emissions from transportation. By eliminating the use of internal combustion engines, electric cars help decrease air pollution. Innovations like solar-powered EVs are emerging, where solar panels on the vehicle can generate additional energy, further enhancing sustainability.

3. **Innovative Transportation Solutions**: Beyond personal vehicles, advancements in solar-powered public transportation, such as solar trains and buses, are also being developed. These systems can operate efficiently while minimizing their environmental footprint.

4.5.2 Recycling and Reusing Materials

1. **Waste Reduction**: Recycling involves processing used materials to create new products, which helps reduce waste in landfills and conserves natural resources. By recycling items like paper, plastic, glass, and metals, communities can significantly lower their environmental impact.
2. **Creative Reuse**: Beyond traditional recycling, reusing materials in innovative ways can further minimize waste. For example, upcycling old furniture or using discarded materials for art projects not only reduces waste but also promotes creativity and resourcefulness.
3. **Circular Economy**: Emphasizing a circular economy encourages businesses and consumers to rethink how products are made and used. This model focuses on designing products for longevity and recyclability, ensuring that materials are continuously reused rather than discarded.

4.5.3 Green Jobs Creating Opportunities

1. **Job Creation in Sustainability**: The transition to a sustainable economy is generating a wide range of job opportunities. Green jobs encompass various sectors such as renewable energy, energy efficiency, waste management, and sustainable agriculture.
2. **Skills Development**: As industries evolve to meet sustainability goals, there is a growing demand for skilled workers trained in green technologies. Educational programs focused on sustainability prepare individuals for these emerging job markets.
3. **Community Benefits**: Green jobs often provide local employment opportunities that contribute to community development. By investing in sustainable practices, communities can enhance their economic resilience while addressing environmental challenges.

4. **Innovation and Entrepreneurship**: The push for sustainability fosters innovation and entrepreneurship as individuals develop new solutions to environmental problems. Startups focused on clean technology or sustainable products are increasingly gaining traction.

In conclusion, leveraging new inventions like solar panels and electric cars, promoting recycling and reuse practices, and fostering green job creation are essential steps toward building a sustainable future. By embracing these innovations and practices collectively, we can protect our planet while creating opportunities for everyone. **Table 4.2** presents innovative strategies for a sustainable future.

Table 4.2: Innovative Methods for a Sustainable Future.

Method	Description	Benefits	Challenges
Using New Inventions to Protect the Planet	**Solar Panels**: Convert sunlight into electricity, providing renewable energy and reducing reliance on fossil fuels. Integration with electric vehicles (EVs) enhances efficiency and sustainability. **Electric Cars**: Reduce greenhouse gas emissions and air pollution by eliminating internal combustion engines. Solar-powered EVs further enhance sustainability. **Innovative Transportation Solutions**: Solar-powered public transportation systems like trains and buses minimize environmental footprint.	- Reduces reliance on fossil fuels - Decreases greenhouse gas emissions - Promotes sustainable transportation	- High initial costs - Technological limitations - Infrastructure requirements
Recycling	**Waste Reduction**:	- Reduces	- Requires

and Reusing Materials	Recycling processes used materials to create new products, reducing landfill waste and conserving natural resources. **Creative Reuse**: Upcycling old furniture or using discarded materials for art projects promotes creativity and resourcefulness while minimizing waste. **Circular Economy**: Focuses on designing products for longevity and recyclability, ensuring continuous reuse of materials.	landfill waste - Conserves natural resources - Encourages creativity and resourcefulness	public participation - Potential contamination of recyclables - Economic feasibility
Green Jobs Creating Opportunities	**Job Creation in Sustainability**: Transition to a sustainable economy generates jobs in renewable energy, energy efficiency, waste management, and sustainable agriculture. **Skills Development**: Growing demand for skilled workers in green technologies. Educational programs prepare individuals for emerging job markets. **Community Benefits**: Green jobs provide local employment opportunities, enhancing economic resilience and addressing	- Generates employment - Promotes economic resilience - Encourages innovation and entrepreneurship	- Need for specialized training - Market competition - Policy and regulatory challenges

environmental challenges.

Innovation and Entrepreneurship: Sustainability fosters innovation and entrepreneurship, with startups focusing on clean technology and sustainable products.

4.6 How Technology Can Help the SDGs

Technology plays a vital role in advancing the Sustainable Development Goals (SDGs) by providing innovative solutions to complex global challenges. Following sections detail that how technology can help achieve these goals through tracking progress, smart urban planning, and innovations in various sectors.

4.6.1 Using Tools Like Apps and Data to Track and Improve Progress

1. **Data Collection and Analysis**: Technology enables the collection of vast amounts of data related to the SDGs. Apps and platforms can gather information on health, education, and environmental conditions, allowing for real-time monitoring of progress toward specific goals.
2. **Mobile Applications**: Various mobile apps are designed to help individuals and communities track their sustainability efforts. For example, apps can monitor energy consumption, waste production, or carbon footprints, empowering users to make informed decisions that contribute to the SDGs.
3. **AI and Big Data**: Artificial intelligence (AI) and big data analytics can identify trends and patterns in data, helping governments and organizations make evidence-based decisions. This can enhance resource allocation and improve the effectiveness of programs aimed at achieving the SDGs.
4. **Public Dashboards**: Governments and organizations can create public dashboards that display progress on SDG targets. These dashboards increase transparency and accountability, encouraging stakeholders to engage in sustainable practices.

4.6.2 Smart Technology for Cities to Use Resources Wisely

1. **Smart City Solutions**: Implementing smart technologies in urban areas can optimize resource use. For instance, smart grids manage electricity distribution more efficiently, reducing waste and lowering emissions.
2. **Intelligent Transportation Systems**: Smart traffic management systems can reduce congestion and pollution by optimizing traffic flow based on real-time data. This not only improves air quality but also enhances urban mobility.
3. **Waste Management Innovations**: Technology can improve waste management through smart bins that monitor fill levels and optimize collection routes, reducing costs and environmental impact.
4. **Water Management Systems**: Smart sensors can detect leaks in water supply systems, ensuring efficient water use and reducing wastage. These systems are essential for achieving SDG 6 (Clean Water and Sanitation).

4.6.3 How Innovation in Healthcare, Farming, and Energy Can Improve Lives

1. **Healthcare Innovations**: Telehealth services have expanded access to medical care, particularly in remote areas. Digital health platforms allow patients to consult with healthcare providers without traveling long distances, improving health outcomes.
2. **Precision Agriculture**: Innovations in farming technology, such as drones and IoT devices, enable farmers to monitor crop health and optimize resource use (water, fertilizers). This leads to increased productivity while minimizing environmental impact.
3. **Renewable Energy Technologies**: Advancements in solar panels, wind turbines, and energy storage solutions are making renewable energy more accessible and affordable. Transitioning to clean energy sources is crucial for combating climate change (SDG 13).
4. **Sustainable Energy Solutions**: Innovations like green hydrogen production offer promising alternatives for energy storage and transportation fuels, contributing to a sustainable energy future.

In conclusion, leveraging technology is essential for driving progress toward the Sustainable Development Goals. By utilizing data-driven tools for tracking progress, implementing smart city solutions for efficient resource management, and fostering innovations in healthcare, agriculture, and energy sectors, we can create a more sustainable future for all.**Table 4.3** presents technological innovations aimed at achieving the Sustainable Development Goals.

Table 4.3: Technological Innovations for Achieving the SDGs.

Method	Description	Benefits	Challenges
Using Tools Like Apps and Data to Track and Improve Progress	**Data Collection and Analysis:** Technology enables the collection of vast amounts of data related to the SDGs. Apps and platforms can gather information on health, education, and environmental conditions, allowing for real-time monitoring of progress toward specific goals. **Mobile Applications:** Various mobile apps are designed to help individuals and communities track their sustainability efforts. For example, apps can monitor energy consumption, waste production, or carbon footprints, empowering users to make informed decisions that contribute to the SDGs. **AI and Big Data:** Artificial	- Real-time monitoring - Informed decision-making - Increased transparency and accountability	- Data privacy concerns - High implementation costs - Need for technical expertise

	intelligence (AI) and big data analytics can identify trends and patterns in data, helping governments and organizations make evidence-based decisions. This can enhance resource allocation and improve the effectiveness of programs aimed at achieving the SDGs. **Public Dashboards:** Governments and organizations can create public dashboards that display progress on SDG targets. These dashboards increase transparency and accountability, encouraging stakeholders to engage in sustainable practices.		
Smart Technology for Cities to Use Resources Wisely	Smart City Solutions: Implementing smart technologies in urban areas can optimize resource use. For instance, smart grids manage electricity distribution more efficiently, reducing waste and lowering emissions. Intelligent Transportation	- Optimized resource use - Reduced emissions and pollution - Enhanced urban mobility	- High initial investment - Maintenance and technical support - Integration with existing infrastructure

	Systems: Smart traffic management systems can reduce congestion and pollution by optimizing traffic flow based on real-time data. This not only improves air quality but also enhances urban mobility. Waste Management Innovations: Technology can improve waste management through smart bins that monitor fill levels and optimize collection routes, reducing costs and environmental impact. Water Management Systems: Smart sensors can detect leaks in water supply systems, ensuring efficient water use and reducing wastage. These systems are essential for achieving SDG 6 (Clean Water and Sanitation).		
How Innovation in Healthcare, Farming, and Energy Can Improve Lives	**Healthcare Innovations:** Telehealth services have expanded access to medical care, particularly in remote areas. Digital health platforms allow	- Improved healthcare access - Increased agricultural productivity - Enhanced energy sustainability	- Technological adoption barriers - High costs of advanced technologies - Need for regulatory support

patients to consult with healthcare providers without traveling long distances, improving health outcomes.

Precision Agriculture:

Innovations in farming technology, such as drones and IoT devices, enable farmers to monitor crop health and optimize resource use (water, fertilizers). This leads to increased productivity while minimizing environmental impact.

Renewable Energy Technologies:

Advancements in solar panels, wind turbines, and energy storage solutions are making renewable energy more accessible and affordable.

Transitioning to clean energy sources is crucial for combating climate change (SDG 13).

Sustainable Energy Solutions:

Innovations like green hydrogen production offer promising alternatives for energy storage and transportation fuels, contributing to a sustainable energy future.

Chapter Highlights

Understanding the SDGs

- Individuals can contribute to achieving the SDGs by taking simple daily actions such as conserving water, reducing waste, using reusable bags and containers, and supporting eco-friendly products.

Volunteering and Education

- Volunteering time can be used to support local community projects or organizations focused on sustainability and social issues.

- Education about the SDGs can inspire others to think about their own actions and how they can help.

- Advocate for change by speaking up about important issues in your community and attending local meetings or writing to representatives about policies that support sustainability and social justice.

Participating in Local Initiatives

- Participating in local initiatives like tree planting events or community clean-ups can help improve the environment and contribute directly to goals related to climate action and sustainability.

- Donating money or resources to organizations working towards specific SDGs can also help.

Continuous Learning and Participation in Relevant Campaigns

- Continuous learning about sustainability issues and participating in relevant campaigns or movements aligns with one's values helps keep important topics alive in the community.

Sustainable Development as a Multifaceted Approach

- Individuals can promote sustainability by actively participating in their communities, raising awareness about social and environmental issues, adopting sustainable lifestyles, supporting local economies, and participating in grassroots movements.

- Companies can contribute to sustainability by implementing sustainable practices, promoting eco-friendly products, fostering corporate social responsibility, building trust through transparency, and collaborating with other businesses.

Collaboration between Individuals, Businesses, and Governments

- Collaboration between individuals, businesses, and governments is essential for driving sustainability and positive change.
- Governments can facilitate large-scale changes through policy-making and regulation.

Involvement in Local and Global Projects

- Communities can start local projects by identifying local needs, engaging community members in the planning process, forming partnerships with local schools, businesses, non-profits, and government agencies, developing action plans, implementing projects, monitoring and evaluating the impact of the projects, and sharing success stories.
- Communities can also collaborate with other businesses to share resources and knowledge about sustainability practices, leading to greater collective impact and encouraging innovation.

The 2030 Agenda for Sustainable Development Goals (SDGs)

- Factors Influencing Progress
- Economic disparities, climate change, political instability, lack of coordination, and data collection issues could slow progress.
- Future iterations of the SDGs may need revisions to address these issues.
- Future iterations might place greater emphasis on inclusivity and technology integration.

Working Faster and Smarter

- Urgency of action, efficiency in resource use, collaboration across sectors, monitoring progress, and engagement of youth and communities are essential for accelerating progress towards the SDGs.
- Regular assessments help ensure initiatives remain aligned with evolving needs and challenges.

The Concept of a Sustainable Future

- The concept of a sustainable future involves a combination of innovative technologies and practices, such as solar panels, electric cars, recycling, and green jobs.

- Solar panels convert sunlight into electricity, providing renewable energy and reducing reliance on fossil fuels.
- Innovative transportation solutions like solar-powered public transportation systems operate efficiently while minimizing their environmental footprint.
- The circular economy model encourages businesses and consumers to rethink how products are made and used, ensuring materials are continuously reused.

Green Jobs and Community Benefits

- Green jobs create opportunities in renewable energy, energy efficiency, waste management, and sustainable agriculture.
- Community benefits include local employment opportunities that contribute to community development.
- Innovation and entrepreneurship are fostered as individuals develop new solutions to environmental problems.

Role of Technology in Achieving SDGs

- Technology plays a crucial role in advancing the SDGs by providing innovative solutions to complex global challenges.
- Data collection and analysis enable real-time monitoring of progress toward specific goals.
- Smart technology for cities can optimize resource use, reduce waste and emissions, and improve air quality and urban mobility.
- Innovation in healthcare, farming, and energy can improve lives by expanding access to medical care, precision agriculture, renewable energy technologies, and sustainable energy solutions.

5.1 The First Industrial Revolution (IR 1.0): Machines and Steam Power (1760s to early 1800s)

The term **"Industrial Revolution"** refers to a series of significant changes in manufacturing and production processes that began in the late 18th century and continued into the 20th century as shown in **Figure 5.1**. These changes transformed economies from being primarily agrarian and handicraft-based to being dominated by industry and machine manufacturing.

Throughout history, the Industrial Revolutions have transformed the way people live, work, and interact with the environment. Each revolution brought new technologies and innovations, but also new challenges. The Sustainable Development Goals (SDGs), created by the United Nations in 2015, aim to solve global problems like poverty, inequality, and environmental damage. In this chapter, we explain how each Industrial Revolution—from the very first to the one happening today—connects to these important goals for a better future.**Table 5.1**provides a concise and comprehensive overview of each Industrial Revolution, linking its defining characteristics to specific Sustainable Development Goals, enabling readers to understand their historical significance and global impact.

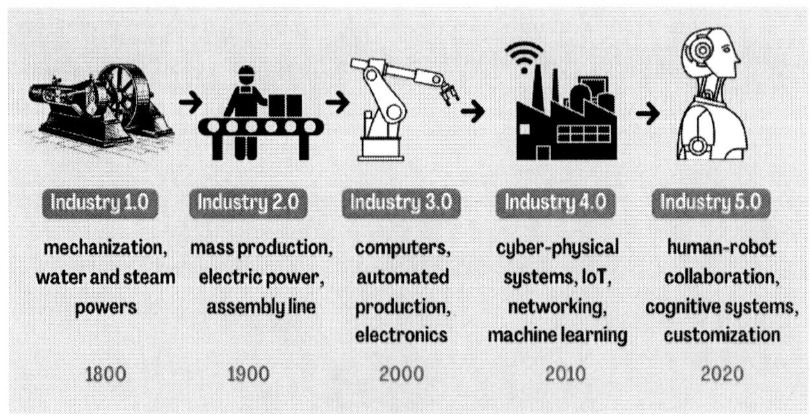

Figure 5.1 Industrial Revolutions.

The First Industrial Revolution was a big change. People moved from farming to working in factories. Machines powered by steam and water made production faster, but working conditions were harsh, cities became overcrowded, and pollution increased.

How It Links to SDGs:

- **Decent Work and Economic Growth (SDG 8):** Factories created jobs, but many workers faced long hours and unsafe conditions.
- **Industry, Innovation, and Infrastructure (SDG 9):** This era marked the beginning of modern industries and new infrastructure like railways.
- **Responsible Consumption and Production (SDG 12):** Mass production began, but people didn't think much about how to use resources wisely.

5.2 The Second Industrial Revolution (IR 2.0): Electricity and Mass Production (Late 1800s to early 1900s)

This revolution introduced electricity, assembly lines, and large-scale production. New inventions like light bulbs and telephones changed everyday life. However, it also led to more factories and bigger cities, increasing pollution and social inequality.

How It Links to SDGs:

- **Affordable and Clean Energy (SDG 7):** Electricity brought power to industries and homes, but it relied on coal, a major polluter.
- **Reduced Inequalities (SDG 10):** While some people became wealthier, many workers were still poor.
- **Sustainable Cities and Communities (SDG 11):** Cities grew quickly but were not planned for long-term sustainability.

5.3 The Third Industrial Revolution (IR 3.0): Computers and the Digital Age (Mid-1900s to late 1900s)

The Third Industrial Revolution introduced computers, the internet, and telecommunications. It made it easier for people to connect, share knowledge, and work more efficiently.

How It Links to SDGs:

- **Quality Education (SDG 4):** Computers made education more accessible, offering new ways to learn.
- **Industry, Innovation, and Infrastructure (SDG 9):** This era built the digital networks and systems we use today.

- **Peace, Justice, and Strong Institutions (SDG 16):** Digital tools improved transparency and accountability in governments and businesses.

5.4 The Fourth Industrial Revolution (IR 4.0): Smart Technologies (2000s to present)

This revolution is all about smart technologies like robots, artificial intelligence (AI), and the Internet of Things (IoT). Machines can now think, learn, and communicate. Factories are becoming smarter, and cities are getting more connected.

How It Links to SDGs:

- **Decent Work and Economic Growth (SDG 8):** New technologies create high-skill jobs but can also replace some traditional jobs.
- **Climate Action (SDG 13):** Smart technologies help track and reduce carbon emissions.
- **Partnerships for the Goals (SDG 17):** Technologies allow better global collaboration.

5.5 The Fifth Industrial Revolution (IR 5.0): Humans and Machines Working Together (The Near Future)

The Fifth Industrial Revolution focuses on people working side by side with advanced machines. It aims to create more personalized and environmentally friendly products.

How It Links to SDGs:

- **Good Health and Well-being (SDG 3):** Advanced technologies are improving healthcare and creating personalized treatments.
- **Industry, Innovation, and Infrastructure (SDG 9):** Industries are moving towards sustainable practices.
- **Life on Land (SDG 15):** Efforts are being made to make production processes more friendly to nature and wildlife.

5.6 The Sixth Industrial Revolution (IR 6.0): Sustainability at the Core

This revolution focuses on making industries sustainable and resilient. It promotes recycling, renewable energy, and preparing for global crises like pandemics or climate change.

How It Links to SDGs:

- **Clean Water and Sanitation (SDG 6):** Innovations are helping save water and treat waste better.
- **Responsible Consumption and Production (SDG 12):** Emphasis on reusing materials and reducing waste.
- **Life Below Water (SDG 14):** Technologies aim to reduce pollution in oceans and protect marine life.

5.7 The Seventh Industrial Revolution (IR 7.0): A Future of Regeneration

The Seventh Industrial Revolution is about going beyond sustainability to actually heal the planet. New technologies like quantum computing and biotechnology will aim to restore ecosystems and improve everyone's quality of life.

How It Links to SDGs:

- **No Poverty (SDG 1):** Technology will help make sure everyone benefits equally from progress.
- **Climate Action (SDG 13):** Revolutionary tools will focus on reversing damage to the climate.
- **Peace, Justice, and Strong Institutions (SDG 16):** New innovations will ensure fair and ethical use of advanced technologies.

Table 5.1: Industrial Revolutions and Their Connection to SDGs.

Revolution	Time Period	Key Features	SDG Relevance
First Industrial Revolution (IR 1.0)	1760s to early 1800s	Transition from farming to factory work; introduction of steam and water-powered machines; increased production, harsh working conditions, and urban overcrowding.	**- SDG 8 (Decent Work and Economic Growth):** Created jobs, but with poor working conditions. **- SDG 9 (Industry, Innovation, and Infrastructure):** Beginnings of modern industries. **- SDG 12 (Responsible Consumption and Production):** Mass production started with limited focus on

			resource efficiency.
Second Industrial Revolution (IR 2.0)	Late 1800s to early 1900s	Introduction of electricity, assembly lines, and large-scale production; innovations like light bulbs and telephones; urban expansion, pollution, and social inequality.	- **SDG 7 (Affordable and Clean Energy)**: Electricity brought widespread power but relied on polluting coal. - **SDG 10 (Reduced Inequalities)**: Wealth gaps persisted. - **SDG 11 (Sustainable Cities and Communities)**: Rapid, unplanned urban growth.
Third Industrial Revolution (IR 3.0)	Mid-1900s to late 1900s	Rise of computers, the internet, and telecommunications; enhanced global connectivity and efficiency in work and knowledge sharing.	- **SDG 4 (Quality Education)**: Made education more accessible. - **SDG 9 (Industry, Innovation, and Infrastructure)**: Established digital systems. - **SDG 16 (Peace, Justice, and Strong Institutions)**: Improved transparency and accountability.
Fourth Industrial Revolution (IR 4.0)	2000s to present	Emergence of smart technologies like AI, IoT, and robotics; smarter factories and more connected cities; focus on automation and data-driven systems.	- **SDG 8 (Decent Work and Economic Growth)**: Created high-skill jobs but replaced traditional roles. - **SDG 13 (Climate Action)**: Enabled carbon tracking and reduction. - **SDG 17 (Partnerships for the Goals)**: Enhanced global collaboration.
Fifth	Near	Collaboration between	- **SDG 3 (Good Health**

Industrial Revolution (IR 5.0)	Future	humans and advanced machines; focus on personalized and eco-friendly production; emphasis on ethical applications of technology.	**and Well-being):** Improved healthcare with personalized treatments. - **SDG 9 (Industry, Innovation, and Infrastructure):** Shift to sustainable practices. - **SDG 15 (Life on Land):** Nature-friendly production processes.
Sixth Industrial Revolution (IR 6.0)	Future	Focus on sustainability and resilience; emphasis on recycling, renewable energy, and crisis preparedness for pandemics or climate change.	- **SDG 6 (Clean Water and Sanitation):** Innovations in water saving and waste treatment. - **SDG 12 (Responsible Consumption and Production):** Focus on material reuse. - **SDG 14 (Life Below Water):** Reduced ocean pollution and marine protection.
Seventh Industrial Revolution (IR 7.0)	Far Future	Aiming for planetary regeneration; use of quantum computing and biotechnology to restore ecosystems and improve life quality; beyond sustainability to proactive regeneration.	- **SDG 1 (No Poverty):** Ensures equitable progress for all. - **SDG 13 (Climate Action):** Tools for reversing climate damage. - **SDG 16 (Peace, Justice, and Strong Institutions):** Ethical use of advanced innovations.

Thus, from the steam engines of the First Industrial Revolution to the smart and sustainable technologies of today, each revolution has shaped the world we live in. Earlier revolutions often focused only on growth and progress, but recent ones are prioritizing sustainability and fairness. By aligning technological advancements with the SDGs, we can create a future where everyone thrives while protecting our planet.

Chapter Highlights

- The Industrial Revolution (IR) transformed economies from agrarian to industrial, introducing new technologies and challenges.
- The SDGs, created by the UN in 2015, aim to address global issues like poverty, inequality, and environmental damage.
- The First Industrial Revolution (IR 1.0) introduced machines and steam power, leading to faster production but harsh working conditions and increased pollution.
- The Second Industrial Revolution (IR 2.0) introduced electricity and mass production, leading to more factories and bigger cities, increasing pollution and social inequality.
- The Third Industrial Revolution (IR 3.0) introduced computers, the internet, and telecommunications, making it easier for people to connect, share knowledge, and work more efficiently.
- The Fourth Industrial Revolution (IR 4.0) focused on smart technologies like robots, AI, and the Internet of Things (IoT), linking to SDGs such as decent work and economic growth, Climate Action, and Partnerships for the Goals.
- The Fifth Industrial Revolution (IR 5.0) focuses on humans and machines working together, aiming to create more personalized and environmentally friendly products.
- The Sixth Industrial Revolution (IR 6.0) focuses on making industries sustainable and resilient.
- The Seventh Industrial Revolution (IR 7.0) aims for planetary regeneration, using technologies like quantum computing and biotechnology to restore ecosystems and improve life quality.